DESIGN MODELLING

Visualising Ideas in 2D and 3D

JOHN BAIRSTOW

ROBERT BARBER

MARILYN KENNY

Hodder & Stoughton

A MEMBER OF THE HODDER HEADLINE GROUP

Preface

Design modelling plays a vital role in the development of any product and covers many different areas of the design process. The focus of the book is to explore the rich variety of methods used to develop design ideas in general design activity.

All aspects of modelling are covered from the initial generation of ideas through rapid visualisation to presenting facsimile models and prototypes. The book is structured to show progression from the simplest modelling techniques to more elaborate replicas. The material is presented in broad progressive sections. The pages are mainly self-contained and can be referred to individually or cross-referenced with others.

Orders: please contact Bookpoint Ltd, 130 Milton Park, Abingdon, Oxon OX14 4SB. Telephone: (44) 01235 827720, Fax: (44) 01235 400454. Lines are open from 9.00 - 6.00, Monday to Saturday, with a 24 hour message answering service. Email address: orders@bookpoint.co.uk

British Library Cataloguing in Publication Data

A catalogue record for this title is available from The British Library

ISBN 0 340 66339 1

First published 1999

Impression number 10 9 8 7 6 5 4

Year 2005

Cover photos supplied by the authors.

Page make-up by Blue Pig Design Co.

Printed in Dubai U.A.E. for Hodder & Stoughton Educational, a division of Hodder Headline Plc, 338 Euston Road, London NW1 3BH by Oriental Press.

ACKNOWLEDGEMENTS

The authors would like to thank the following for their help in the preparation of this book:
Staff and students from the Design courses at Sheffield Hallam University, especially Chris Moon, Sally Hobday, Jim Dawson, Peter Knight, Glyn Hawley, Gordon Young and Peter Kaye.

Steve Kenny – Senior Design Manager Jaguar Cars Ltd, Phil Mellor – Exhibition Designer, Linnel, Robert Naybour, Tony Meadows Architects, James Dyson, Dyson Appliances, Lippa Pearce Design and Pentagram Design Ltd.

We are also grateful to the following for permission to use copyright material:
Simair Ltd, Foster and Partners, architects and designers, LEGO Dacta, Iain Denby, Styles Rapid Prototyping, Julie Verhoeven, Matt Hamant – Brunel University and Thea Penna – Bretton Hall College.

The publishers would like to thank the following for permission to reproduce photographs in this book:
Action Plus; Camerapress; Corbis/Bettmann.

The cartoons were drawn by Dave Blewitt.

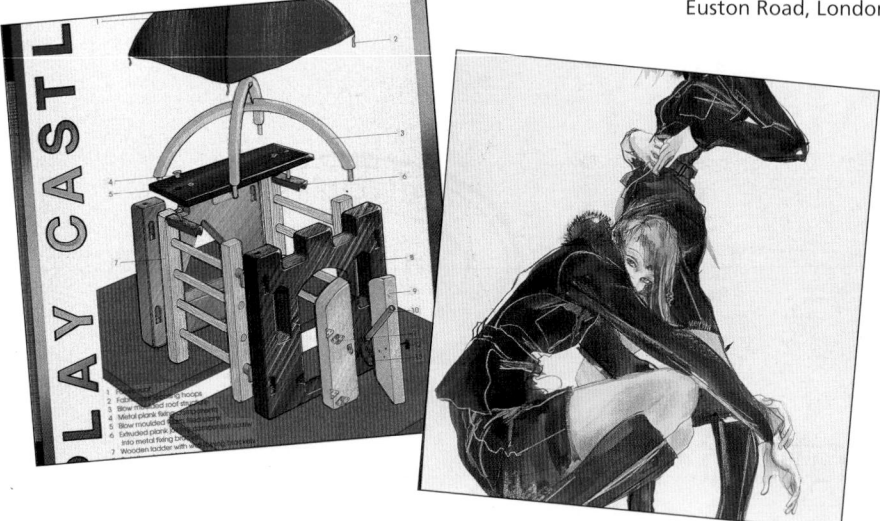

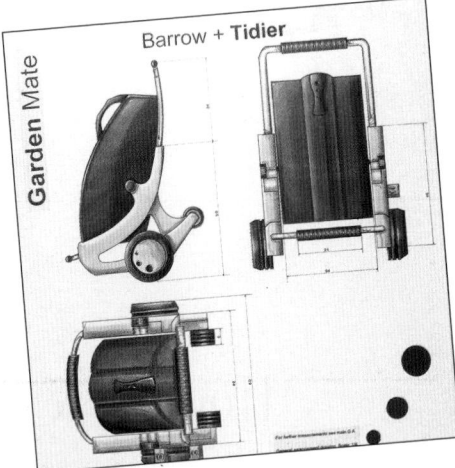

Contents

Getting Started

'We ask what does the user want from the product in real terms? What functions does he/she want? What is his/her lifestyle, what products surround him/her? It's about getting into the minds of the consumer.' DICK POWELL

For many of us, one of the most difficult parts of the design process is getting started. Sitting in front of a blank piece of paper and worrying because you have no ideas will only make things worse. The more you worry about it, the less likely you are to come up with good ideas.

Design does not necessarily start with drawing, particularly if you have no ideas. What you really need to do at the beginning of a project is to investigate the problem thoroughly. For example, if you have been asked to design a letter head for a toy manufacturer, you will need to find out everything you can about the company. This kind of 'finding out' is called **design research**.

DESIGN RESEARCH

This is a very important part of the design process. The more you understand the problem, the better your ideas will be. Design research has two main purposes– firstly to find out as much as possible about the product, and secondly, to gather information that helps you to think creatively.

PRODUCT RESEARCH

A design brief will sometimes include a **design specification**. This is a list of requirements which your proposal must meet if it is to be successful. If you are not provided with such a list, it is a good idea to write one for yourself, as much of your research will be based on it. The majority of things on this list will involve practical needs such as how much it should cost to make your design. However, it is also a good idea to describe the visual or aesthetic qualities of the product (in other words, the impression the product should give e.g. friendly, serious, humorous etc.).

Product research involves finding the answers to a series of questions. For example:

- How big?
- How many?
- What materials?
- Who will use it?
- What are their needs?

The answers to some of these questions will provide clear information that can be used to decide whether or not the design is successful. If you are asked to design a carton to contain half a litre of milk, then the carton must contain exactly that amount. This is very important to the manufacturer – less or more milk would not be acceptable.

There are no 'nearly right' solutions to this type of question. Sometimes it is not so easy to judge whether a product will be successful. The same milk carton may be required to appeal to the teenage market. In this case your research will lead to a number of possibilities rather than an exact solution, and in some cases it is important to understand that not everyone will agree – this is called a **subjective judgement**.

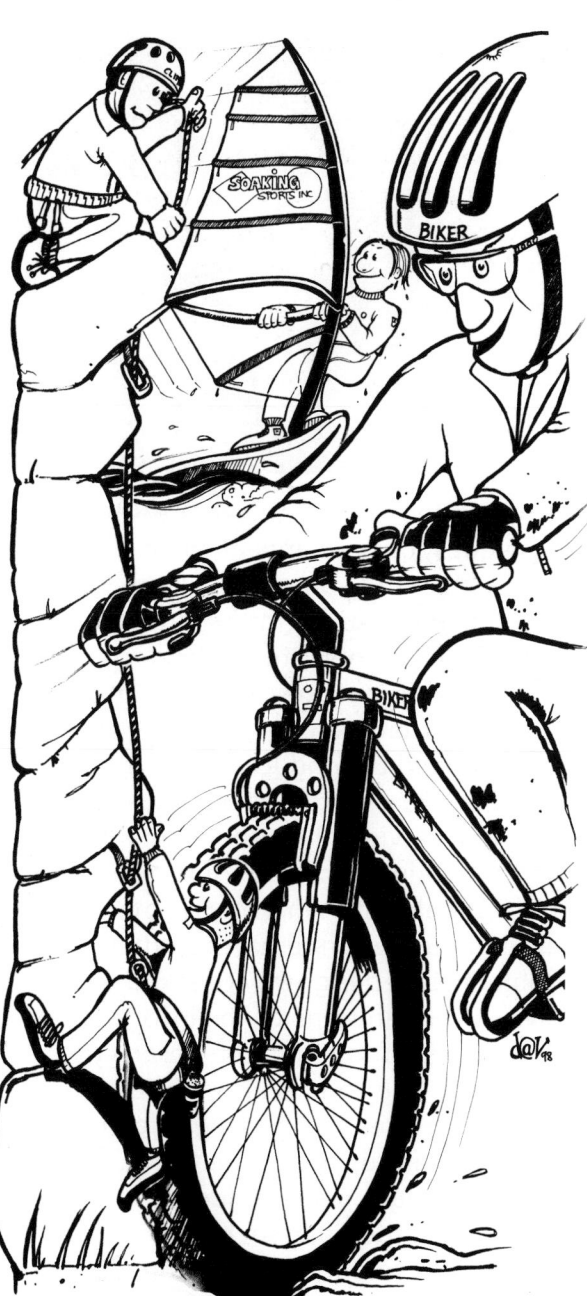

Design Specifications

Design specification: Milk carton for the teenage market

- Must contain half a litre

- Will be mechanically filled and sealed

- Must be easy to open and re-seal

- Must be cheap to manufacture

- Where possible use materials which can be recycled

- Must make effective use of the limited space available in vendor's chiller cabinets

- Must pack efficiently into larger containers for delivery

- Must be capable of withstanding the rough handling experienced during storage and delivery

- Form and style of the container should appeal to a health-conscious teenage market

- Container should also appeal to parents of teenagers and other potential buyers of product

- Container should present a clean and fresh image (similar to other milk-based products).

Although looking for the answers to all these questions can appear to be impossible, once you get involved with the problem it can be interesting and rewarding. You need to develop many different skills and may find strengths you never knew you had. In some cases you will need to conduct workshop experiments, whilst in others you may need to interview the people who will use the product. These are just examples. There are almost as many ways of carrying out design research as there are problems that designers are asked to solve. Although some of the information needed can be found in the library, you will often need to find information from 'primary sources', such as manufacturers and materials suppliers. The technology used to produce new products is changing all the time, so, by the time the relevant information reaches the library, it may well be out of date.

'Design is not about genius. It is about cardboard and sticky tape, borrowing ideas and testing every detail until it works.' JAMES DYSON

People are naturally inventive, however, there are many things that prevent us from thinking creatively. Worrying because you can't think of good ideas has already been mentioned. Attempting to solve the problem before you have had the time to think about it is another mistake. You can avoid this by thinking about ways of approaching the problem rather than trying to produce a solution straight away. For example:

- Give the product a name and a character

- Experiment with materials

- Make unlikely combinations, such as 'radio-controlled clothing'

- Transferring technology, e.g. riveting wood

You shouldn't be afraid of experimenting or making mistakes. Don't expect your first ideas to be the best you can do. You will probably find that as you become more familiar with the problem, your ideas will improve. A number of design strategies such as 'brainstorming' are covered in detail on the following pages. By using one or more of these techniques, you will be directing your mind to think in a particular way. The more strategies you use, the greater will be the number and diversity of your ideas.

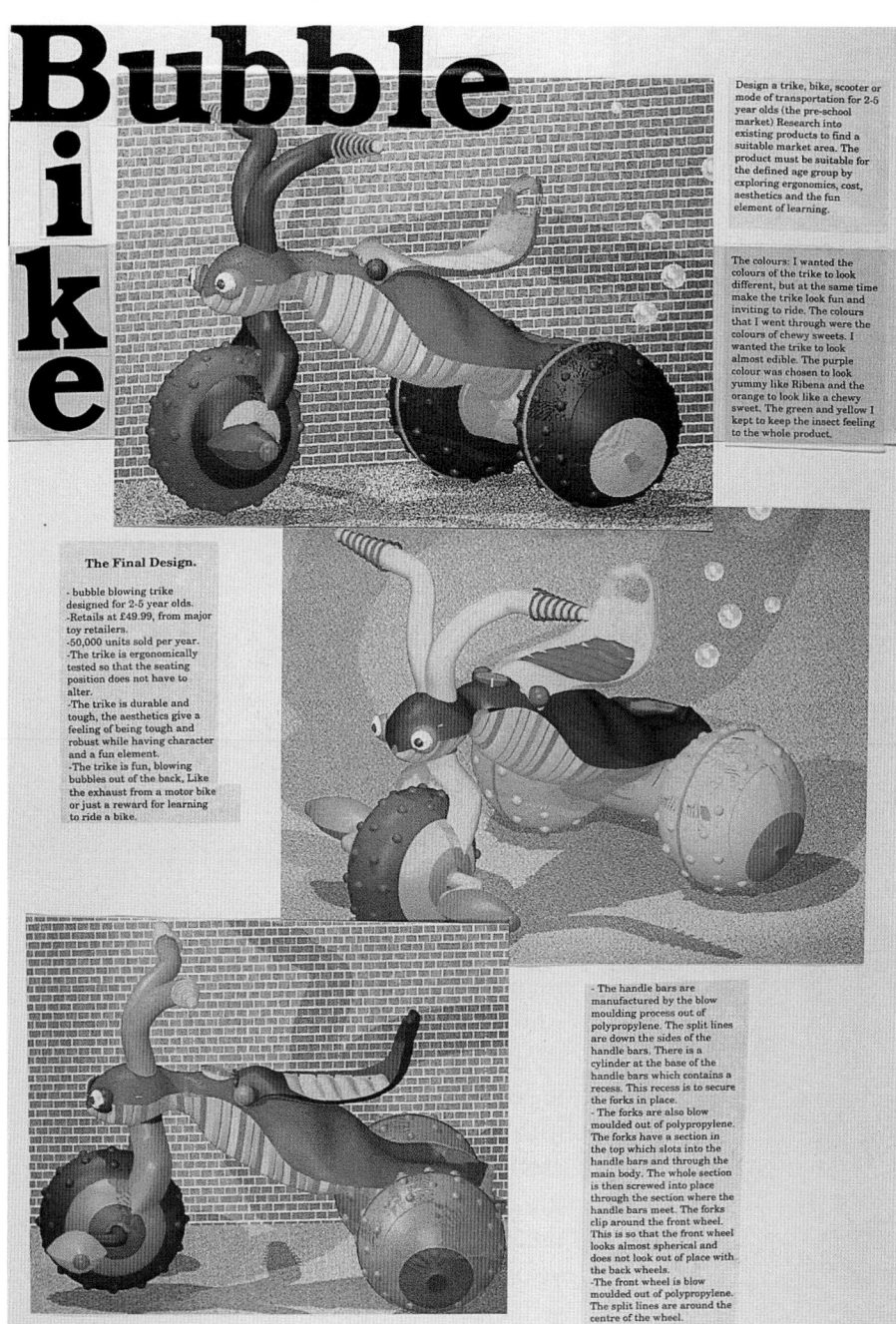

Bubble Bike

Design a trike, bike, scooter or mode of transportation for 2-5 year olds (the pre-school market). Research into existing products to find a suitable market area. The product must be suitable for the defined age group by exploring ergonomics, cost, aesthetics and the fun element of learning.

The colours: I wanted the colours of the trike to look different, but at the same time make the trike look fun and inviting to ride. The colours that I went through were the colours of chewy sweets. I wanted the trike to look almost edible. The purple colour was chosen to look yummy like Ribena and the orange to look like a chewy sweet. The green and yellow I kept to keep the insect feeling to the whole product.

Using a name and character as a starting point

The Final Design.

- bubble blowing trike designed for 2-5 year olds.
- Retails at £49.99, from major toy retailers.
- 50,000 units sold per year.
- The trike is ergonomically tested so that the seating position does not have to alter.
- The trike is durable and tough, the aesthetics give a feeling of being tough and robust while having character and a fun element.
- The trike is fun, blowing bubbles out of the back, Like the exhaust from a motor bike or just a reward for learning to ride a bike.

- The handle bars are manufactured by the blow moulding process out of polypropylene. The split lines are down the sides of the handle bars. There is a cylinder at the base of the handle bars which contains a recess. This recess is to secure the forks in place.
- The forks are also blow moulded out of polypropylene. The forks have a section in the top which slots into the handle bars and through the main body. The whole section is then screwed into place through the section where the handle bars meet. The forks clip around the front wheel. This is so that the front wheel looks almost spherical and does not look out of place with the back wheels.
- The front wheel is blow moulded out of polypropylene. The split lines are around the centre of the wheel.

Creative Thinking

The inspiration for this light came from sketch studies of a Nautilus shell. Card models were used to develop the form of the light

If you are given a brief to design a desk light and only carry out research that involves looking at other lights, you are unlikely to think of anything original. You need to look elsewhere for new ideas. For example, it might be interesting to look at the natural forms created by sea creatures, to see if similar ideas could be used in the design of your desk light. By choosing where to look for your ideas you will be able to control what your design will look like.

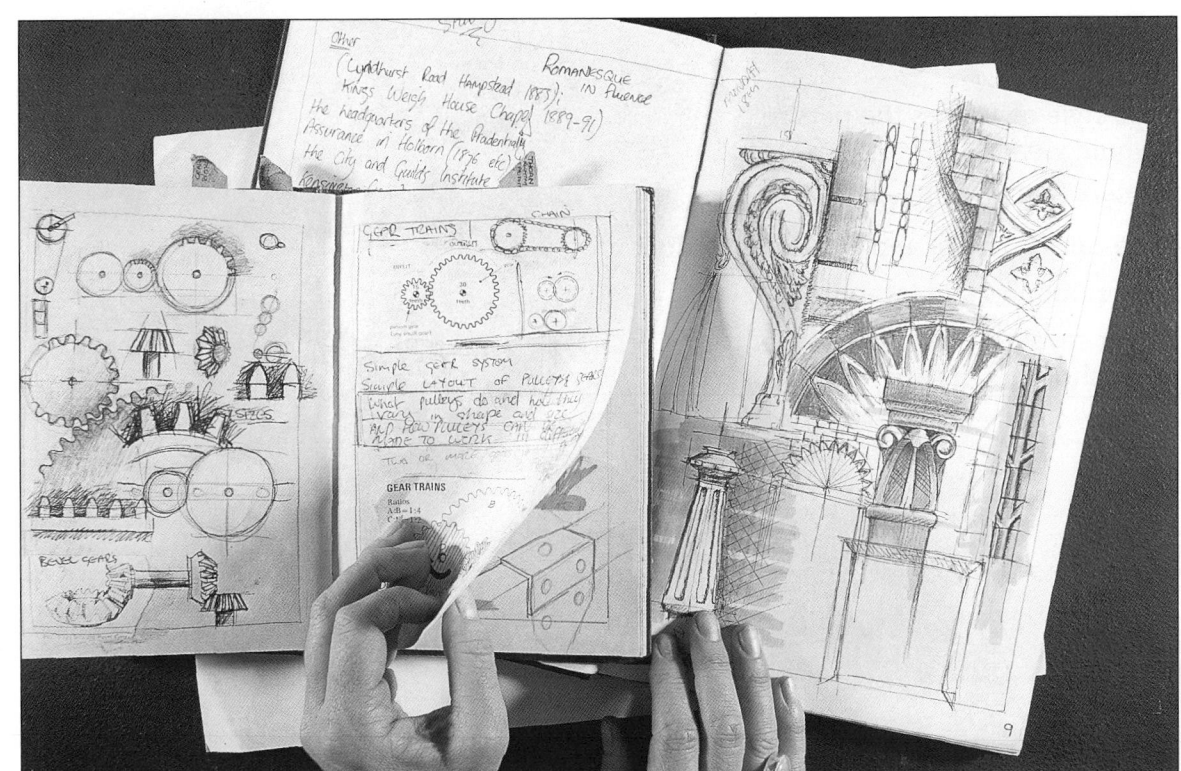

Once set on a particular track, your mind is capable of producing results within a few minutes. On the other hand, it may take several hours or even days. Ideas do not always arrive at a convenient time, therefore it is a good idea to keep a sketch book so that you can note them down ready for development at a later time. Remember Archimedes and his shout of 'Eureka!' whilst getting into his bath? Historians tell us that this was the *exact* moment when he discovered his theory of displacement, though in fact, it is likely that he had been thinking about the problem for some time before.

Image Boards

Once you have your design brief it is important to form a clear idea of the type of person you are designing for. You will then be able to make decisions about the style of the design and the physical needs of the user.

A way of forming a picture of the user is to create an **image board**. This is a collage of sketches and magazine pictures that show the lifestyle of an imaginary person.

An image board might include pictures of:

- the style of clothes the person would wear
- where and how they live
- the car they drive and the job they do
- their hobbies and interests
- their favourite music, restaurants and shops.

Mood boards are similar to image boards but they are not just about the user. They can be collections of colours, textures and cut-outs from magazines that suggest a mood or theme. They are used to help you to give your product an identity.

For example, if you have decided that your design should have a fresh 'sporty' image, then a mood board built up around this theme will instantly give you ideas for colours and shapes that have a sporty quality.

Moodboards suggesting:
Fig. 1 Fresh, sporty image
Fig. 2 French, country living
Fig. 3 Spicy and exotic

1

2

3

User Trips

User trips, as the name suggests, involve carrying out a task in order to understand more about a particular problem. So, if you are asked to design a better ironing board, you may need to do the family ironing for a week or two. If ironing is beyond you, then an alternative is to carry out a **video analysis**. This simply means using a video camera to record an expert at work. Later on you can study the video to get a better understanding of the problem you are trying to solve.

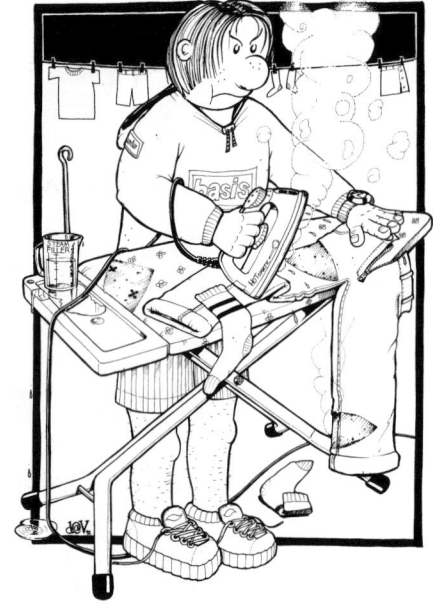

A TYPICAL USER TRIP

Try changing the wheel on a car and ask yourself the following questions:

- Are all the things you need easily accessible – spare wheel, tools, jack, etc.?
- Is the jack easy to use?
- Does it seem to need three hands and a foot to operate it?
- Does the wheel wrench provide enough leverage to slacken the wheel nuts?
- Do you or your clothes get dirty in the process?
- Is the wheel heavy or difficult to handle? Would it be if you were not quite so fit?

Next, imagine performing the same task on a cold and rainy Saturday evening, whilst on the way to a restaurant to celebrate your birthday with your family. Would this make the problem more difficult? How could you make the task easier or less stressful?

When you have the answers to these questions, as well as some of your own, you may be ready to start designing a solution!

Brainstorming is a way of generating a lot of ideas quickly. It works best with a group of people so that you can bounce ideas off each other.

HOW TO BRAINSTORM

- You will need some large pieces of paper and one person to write all the ideas down.

- Start by writing the problem in the centre of the page.

- Call out ideas as they come to you. Set a time limit.

- Try to put down as many ideas as possible in the time allowed, no matter how silly they seem.

The key to brainstorming is that your idea may trigger off a thought in somebody else. Ideas should flow quickly. You will have lots of very different ideas. At the end some will be useful, some will not.

BRAINSTORM SKETCHING

- Stick large pieces of paper on the wall or table.

- Use large felt-tipped pens.

- Draw your ideas very quickly.

- After a minute everyone moves round one place and more drawings are added.

- Repeat this four or five times.

- Add notes to explain your drawing if necessary.

At the end, look at all the sketches and pick out the ideas that have potential.

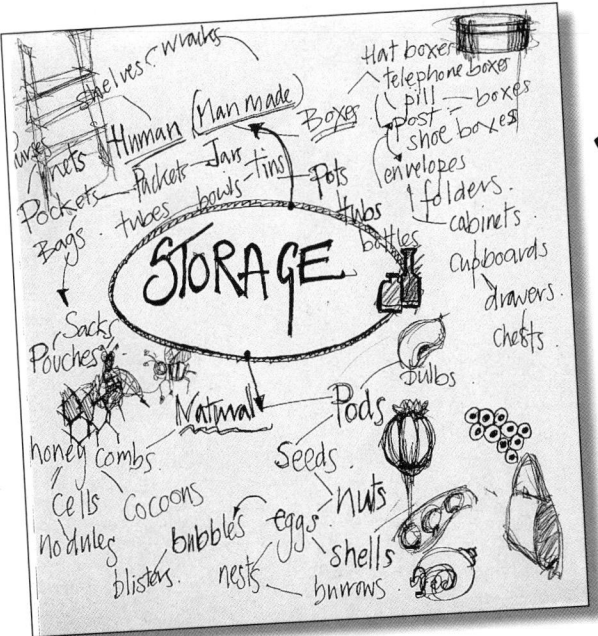

2D Layout

The arrangement of text, image and colour in a two-dimensional design is known as **layout** or **composition**. You must give careful thought to the layout of graphic work to ensure that the design communicates clearly.

Layout is also used to suggest a mood that can reinforce the message in a graphic design. For example, if you want to give a design a serious, calm quality, then the text and shapes could be arranged in a regular and symmetrical form to suggest order. Alternatively, an arrangement that is unbalanced or off-centre may make the viewer feel uncomfortable, but it will also demand attention and seem more dynamic.

You will need to experiment with various layouts (enlarging and reducing shapes, changing colours, altering amount of space, etc.) until you achieve the mood or quality that you want to communicate.

You can use 'modelling' as a technique for exploring 2D designs such as page layouts, poster designs or packaging labels. Although you are not using 3D materials, the process is very similar.

A good starting point is to list or draw all the design elements that have to be included, for example, the headings, text, photographs, illustrations and logos. Listing them in order of priority will give you an idea of size and position – the most important items will probably be largest and most dominant.

Cut out each part to form a block (text can be cut out of a newspaper) and try rearranging them within the overall size of the finished piece. This shuffling about of cut up paper is a very quick way of generating ideas for layout. It is easy to enlarge or reduce shapes on a photocopier. Some of the 'accidents' that happen while you are searching for the 'right design' may be far more inspiring than your first proposals.

If you find it difficult arranging layouts intuitively, you may find it helpful to use a **grid**.

Most 2D design work is based on an underlying grid structure. The grid ensures that there is some unity to a design and that all the different pages in a book or magazine look as if they belong together because they share the same style.

The grid is used as an underlay so that each page has similar margins and columns for text. Photographs and pieces of paper representing text can be placed in various formations over the grid. You can experiment by changing the size of certain items, extending blocks beyond one column or leaving areas blank. Grids used imaginatively can inspire new and unusual layouts.

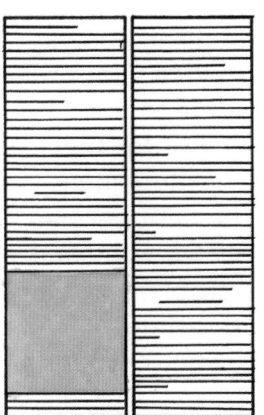
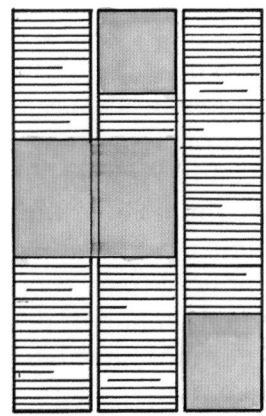
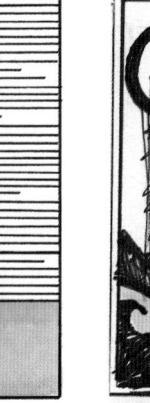

Using Props

Very simple models can act as 'props' that we can handle and play with to stimulate a new way of looking at a problem. In this illustration (below) a designer has used foam blocks to represent the working parts of a radio. The circle, rectangle and square are replacing the speaker, battery and 'guts' of the radio. By moving them about and recording the different arrangement of shapes with simple line drawings, the designer is able to break away from the typical idea of a rectangular radio and explore more unusual possibilities of what a radio could look like.

Here the designer is working on an electronic safety device that would make pedestrians more visible to motorists in the dark. The design uses flashing LEDs (light emitting diodes) that operate with a small battery. A simple foam block has been covered in double-sided tape and placed on different parts of the body. This gives the designer an idea about which position is most visible to the motorist and most convenient for the wearer. Of course, some of these ideas might have occurred if the designer had simply sat down with a sketch book and thought hard about the problem, but a whole range of other interesting solutions have been suggested through experimentation.

Thumbnails are small, rough sketches that can help you to work out design problems on paper. You only need to draw the main parts of the design in the form of a simple diagram. As thumbnails are quick to do, they will not slow down your design thinking. You should be able to produce lots of sketches exploring a wide range of ideas. It is this playing around with ideas that can give inspired design solutions.

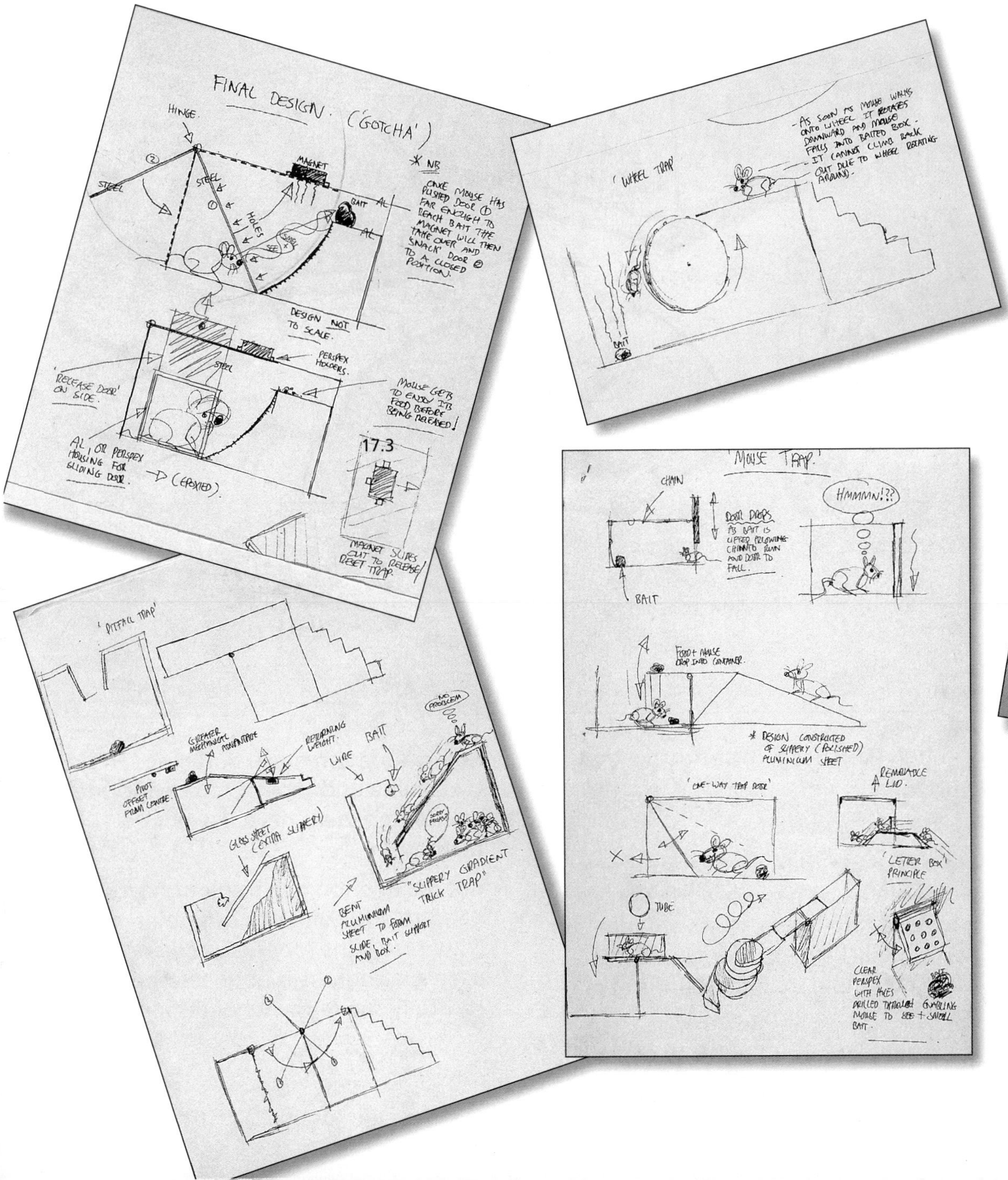

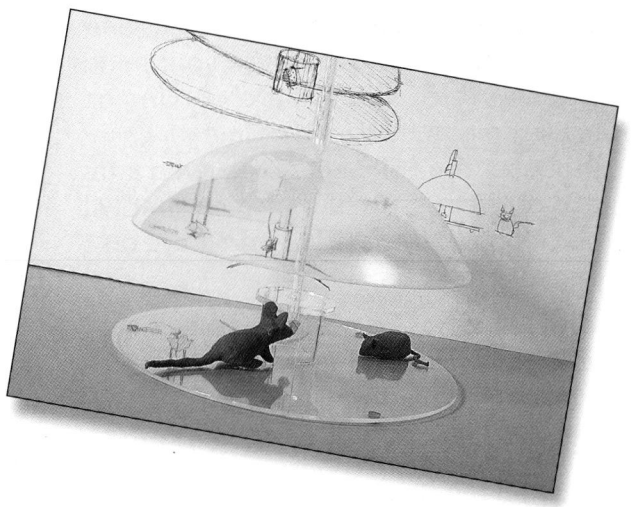

Ideas for a mousetrap

Quick Sketching

As you become more involved in the design and wish to consider your ideas in more depth, or to discuss them with others, you will need to produce larger, slightly more detailed sketches. They act as a useful record of ideas, allowing you to reflect on them or save them for possible development later.

Rough sketches should be quickly produced and spontaneous. They allow you to show your thinking on paper and, although early design ideas will probably be vague, the very act of sketching will force you to make design decisions and define things more clearly in your mind. Often a sketch that you are working on will prompt a new idea or line of thought. You will need to develop a fast and effective style of sketching that will help you catch these fleeting ideas on paper.

Initial sketches do not have to be neat and accurate. It does not matter if a line is not in exactly the 'right place'. Do not stop to rub it out – you can simply draw it in more boldly afterwards. As you become more confident, your sketches will flow and lose any stiff clumsy quality as you adopt a more fluent, spontaneous style.

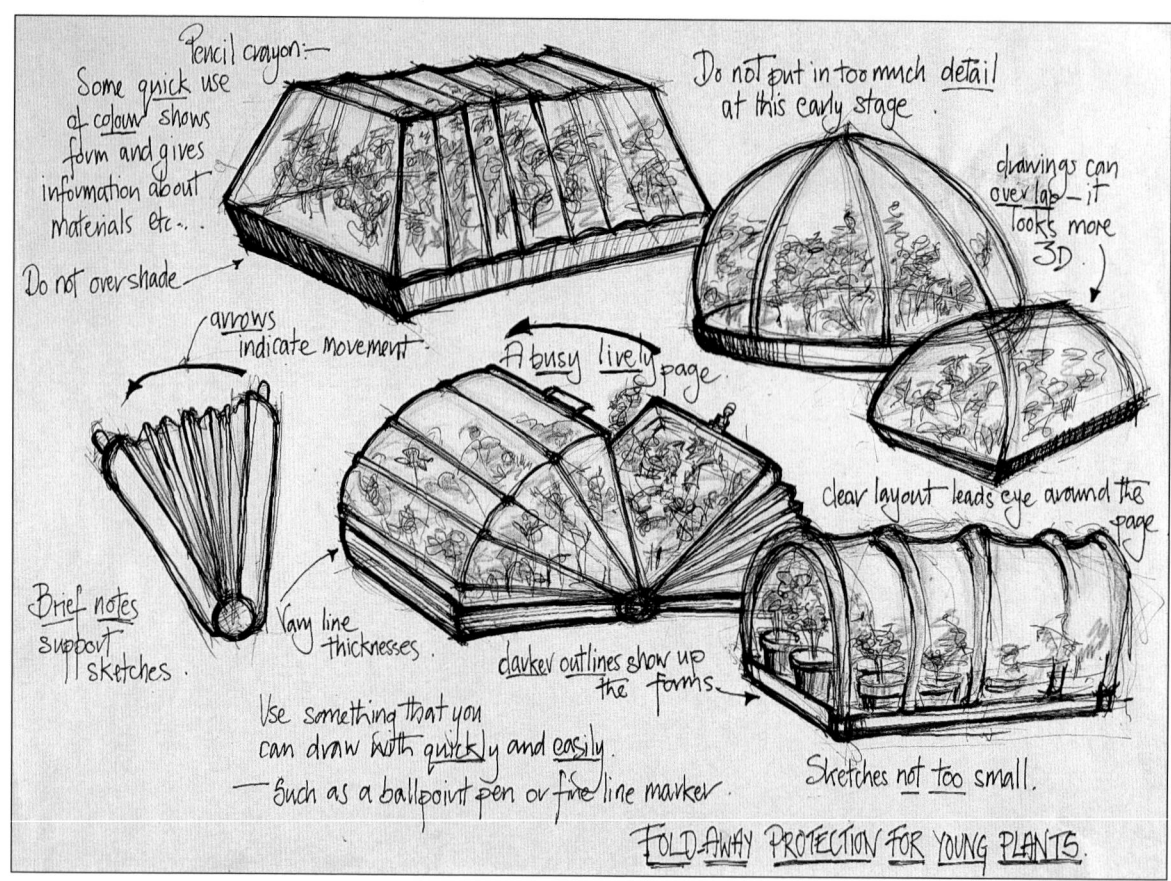

For rough sketches to be effective they should:

- be quickly produced

- use a medium that you feel comfortable with and that is easy to work. Pencils, biros and fine-line markers are ideal for making quick line drawings and for showing simple shading to indicate form

- use arrows and brief notes to explain ideas

- not include too much detailing. This takes time and is better to be included later when ideas have developed further

- not include too much colour. If you need to add colour at this point, pencil crayon or light tones of marker can be used sparingly. It is not necessary to carefully shade the whole thing.

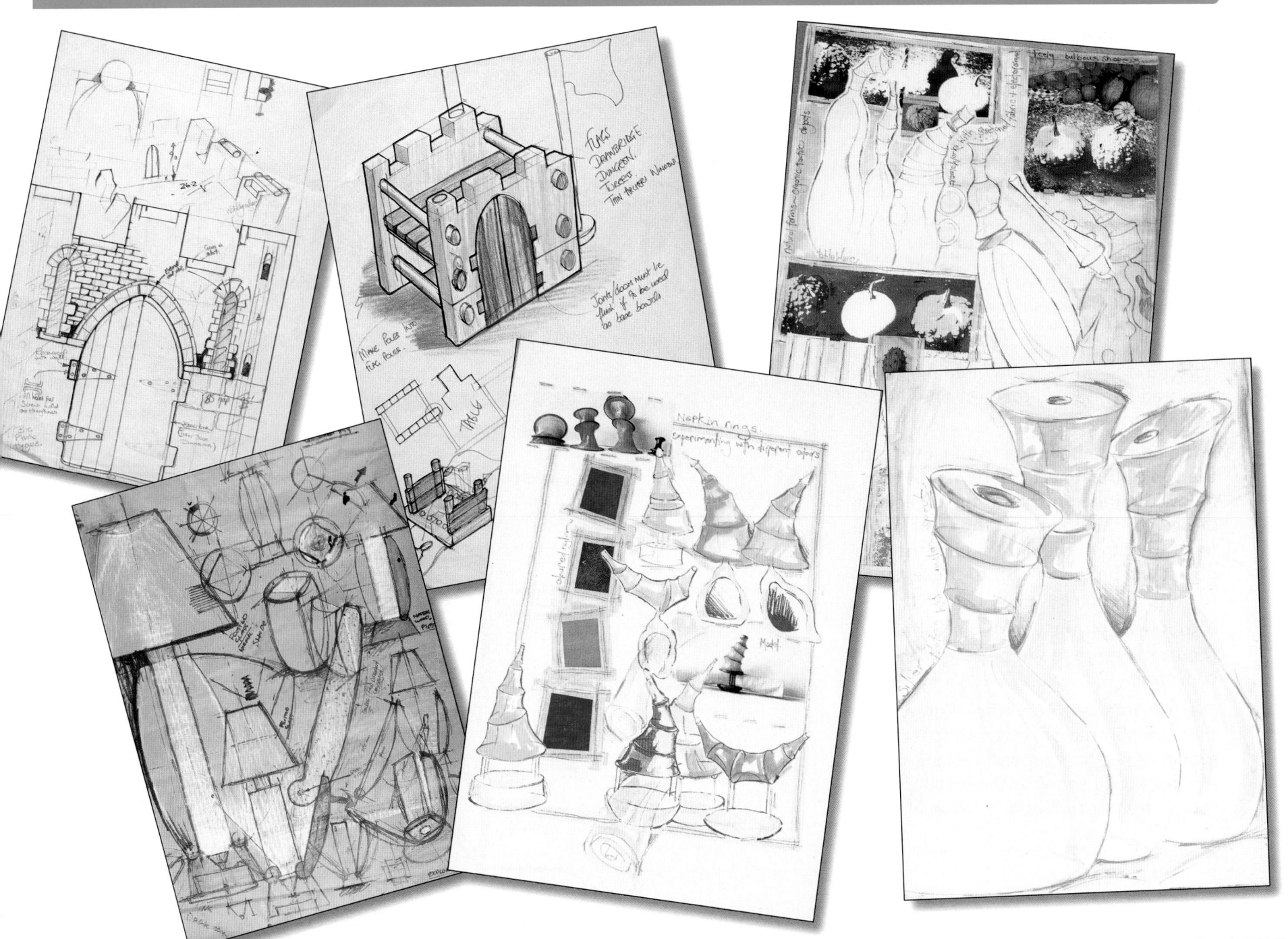

One Point Perspective

It is useful, in the initial stages of designing, to draw a three-dimensional image of your idea. To do this, it will be necessary to come to terms with either one point or two point perspective to create a line drawing.

One point is the simplest form of perspective drawing. The front view is drawn as a flat two-dimensional image with all receding lines taken back to one vanishing point.

The position of the vanishing point will determine the view that you get of the object in the finished drawing and can be adjusted to give you the best one possible for your design.

If the point is above the front view then the top of the object will be seen. If it is below then the bottom of the object will be seen. If the point is to the right of the front view then the right side of the object will be seen. If it is to the left then the left side will be seen.

Also, the closer the vanishing point is to the front view, the sharper the lines will converge.

One advantage of this type of drawing is that complicated or curved shapes can be drawn as flat two-dimensional views. It is also useful for showing the view of a room, street scenes and 'bird's-eye' views.

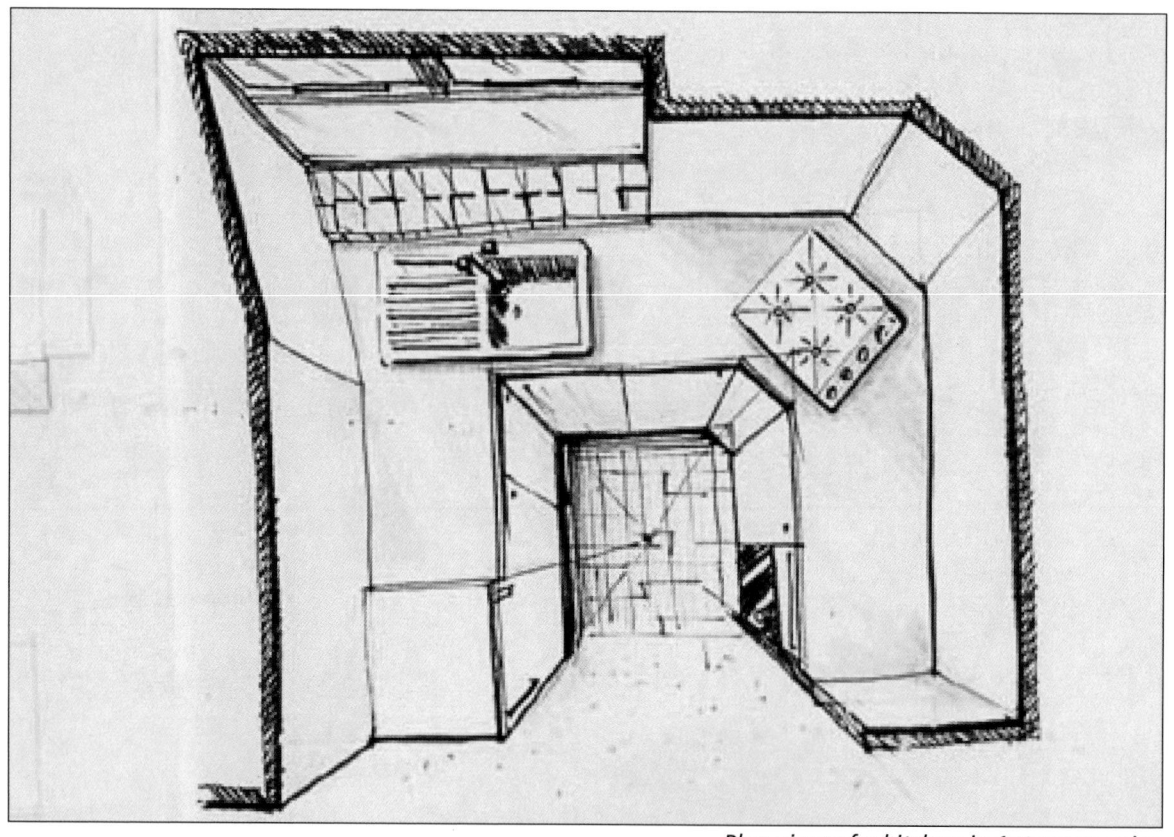

Plan view of a kitchen in 1pt perspective

The most common type of perspective drawing is **two point** and is used extensively to convey a designer's first thoughts about design proposals. When drawing in two-point, the vertical or upright lines remain while all other lines recede to two vanishing points. These points are situated on a horizontal line which is known as the **eye level**. The view you see of the object will be determined by its position in relation to the eye line and its vanishing points. This gives the designer the opportunity to give the drawing the most advantageous impression of the product. For instance, when the object is drawn below the eye line, a view of the top surface will be seen, while the underside is visible when it is placed above the eye line.

To draw out these construction lines every time you want to convey an idea would be time consuming. It can be sketched so that it looks right to the eye even though it may not be 'true' perspective. In developing your two-dimensional modelling skills, it is important to be able to use this method quickly and effectively. It will take practice to come to terms with estimating the perspective lines but will be helpful in drawing out your initial ideas.

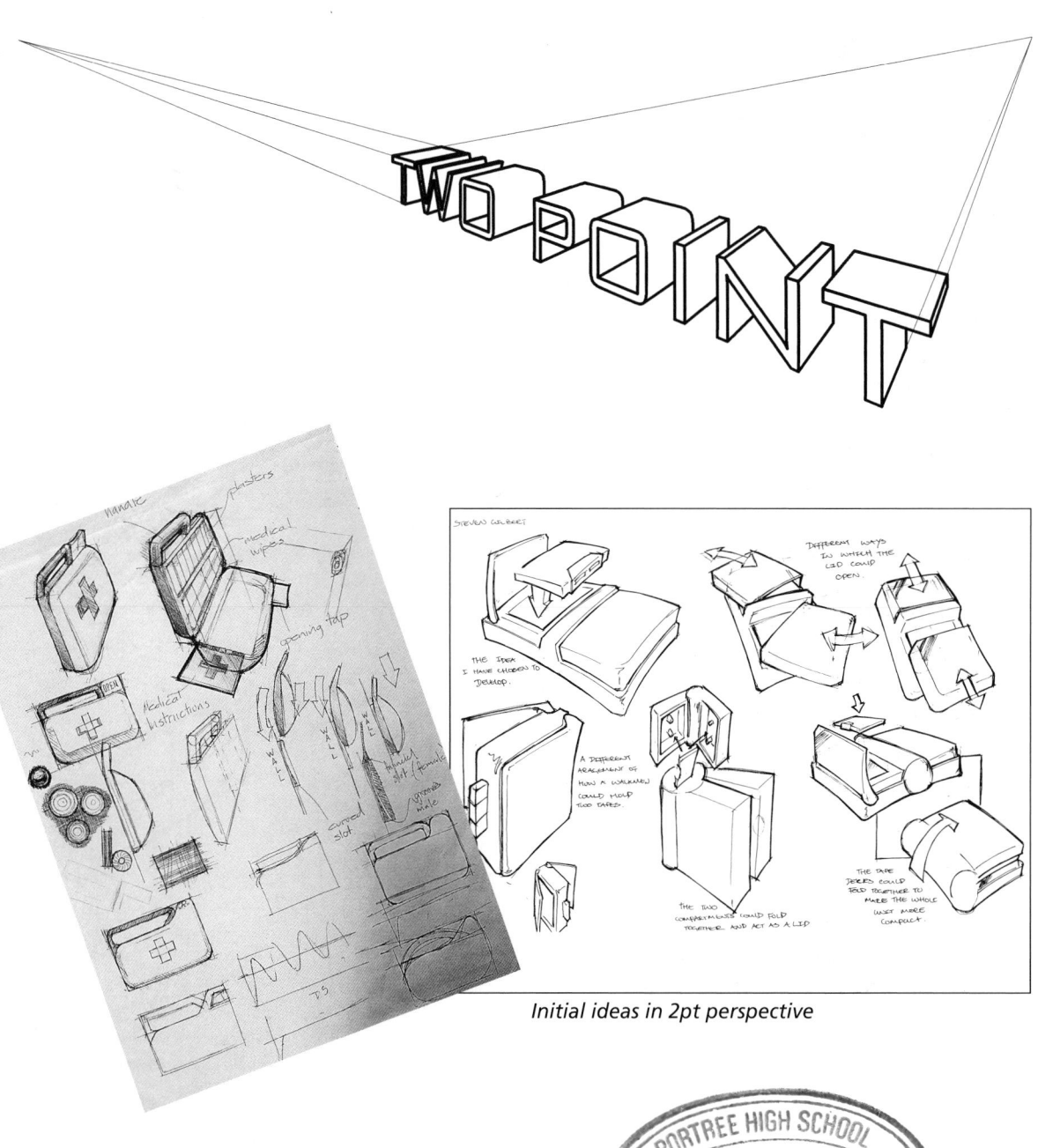

Initial ideas in 2pt perspective

Crating

When attempting this type of drawing, it will probably be easier to imagine the product and its component parts fitting inside a series of boxes or crates. These will be much easier to draw in the initial stages rather than attempting to draw complex curves from scratch. It is also easier to judge a cube when drawing. Using this as a basis, the final shape can be drawn in with relation to these crates.

This example shows a concept for a torch. The torch has curves and ellipses which need to be drawn in perspective. The easiest way to do this is to think of the product as a number of boxes joined together. The ellipses can then be constructed on the face of each box.

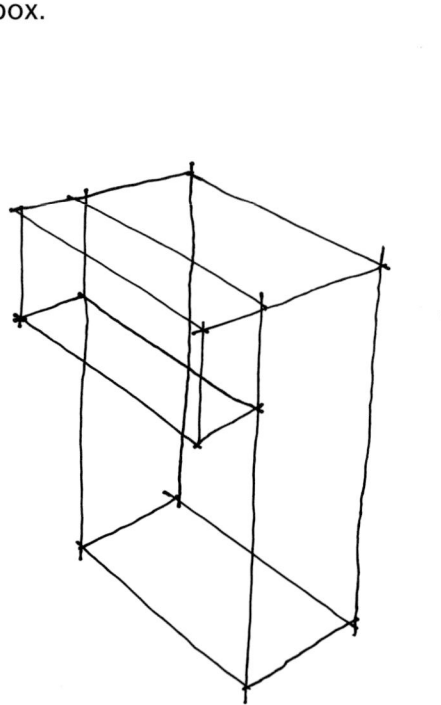
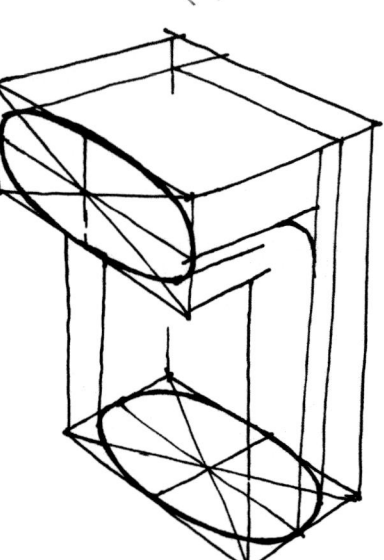

The 'crating' process

You can add shading to a drawing to make an object look three dimensional and more realistic. Before starting to draw you should decide on the direction of light and plan which parts of the object will be the lightest. Remember that all the surfaces nearest to the light source will be the palest. The parts facing away from the light will be in shade and so will look darker. These variations of light and dark are called **tone**.

Shading will vary according to the shape of the item being drawn. For example, a curved surface would show a gradation of tone – gradually blending from light to dark.

The type of material from which the object is made will also affect the quality of the light reflected off it. Smooth, polished surfaces are highly reflective and have extreme contrasts of light and dark tones. Matt surfaces tend to look dull with little variation in tone.

Flat, 'dead'-looking drawings are usually due to poor shading. It is easy to overshade a drawing and make it look 'heavy' with little variation between light and dark.

You can give form to rough sketches by a little quick shading with a pencil crayon or a pale-coloured marker.

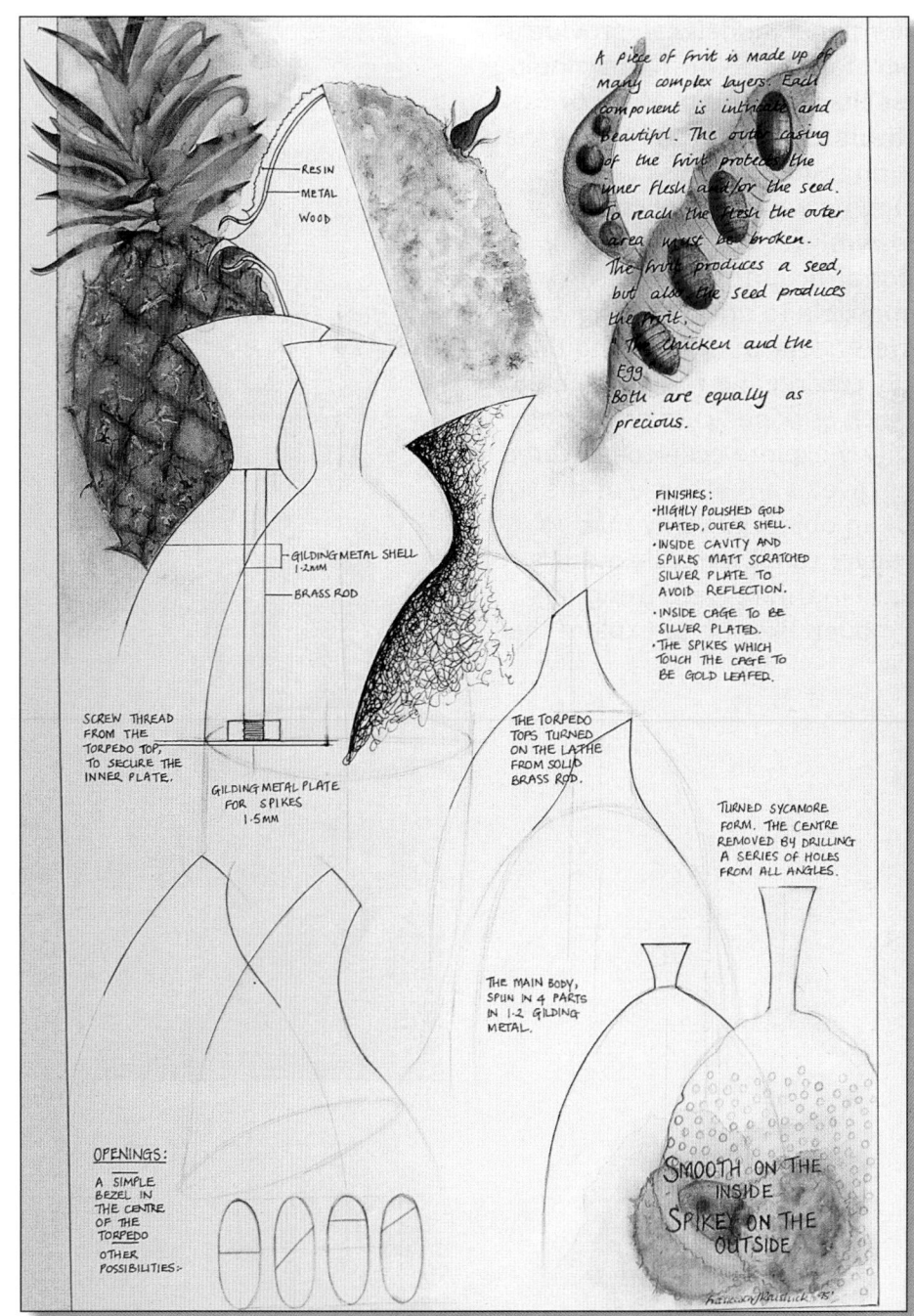

3D Modelling

Three-dimensional models can provide a much easier starting point for developing initial ideas than sketching. Many of us find it difficult to visualise the things that we are trying to design. This is particularly true when complicated shapes are involved. Because we find these things difficult to visualise, they are almost impossible to draw. Making models offers a way of overcoming this problem. By cutting and forming simple materials such as paper, card and wood, we can quickly explore even complicated ideas. They give us a real sense of the size and feel of an object in a way that drawings never can. Even scale models can be useful in this respect. Designers often use models like this to explore their initial ideas.

Student work area showing initial modelling of ideas for a sun lounger

At the early stage of a design it is important to work quickly as you will probably have lots of ideas. This means choosing materials which are easy to work, and which will successfully create the effect you are looking for. Initial models usually deal with one aspect of a design and are therefore quite simple. In this way a block of polystyrene foam may be suitable to explore the form of a camera, whereas stiff wire would be a more suitable choice to study different structures for a metal-framed chair.

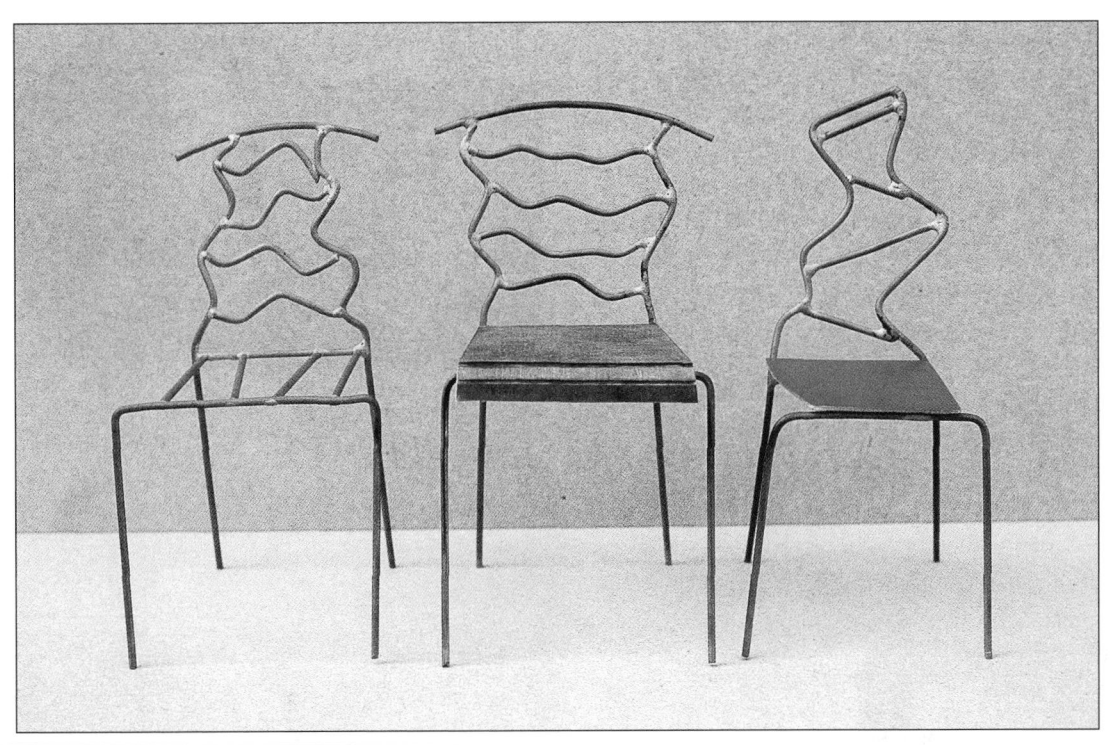

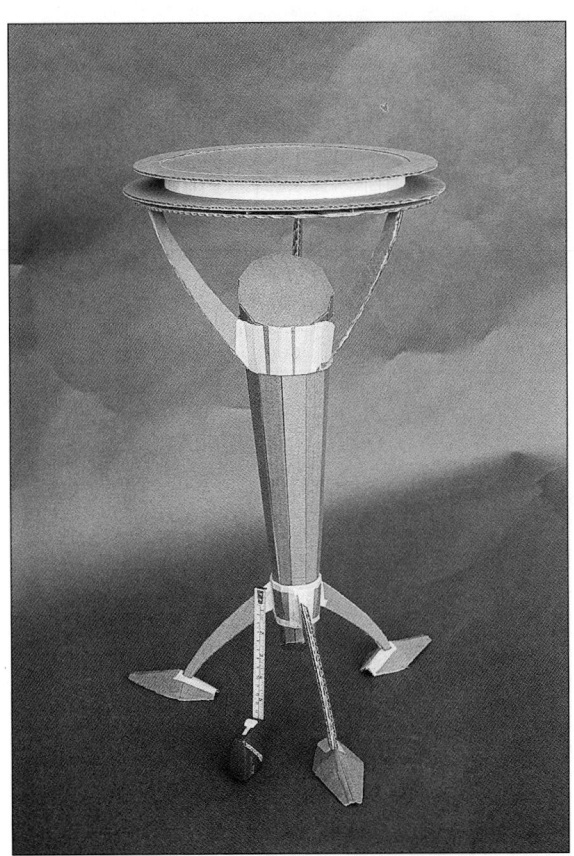

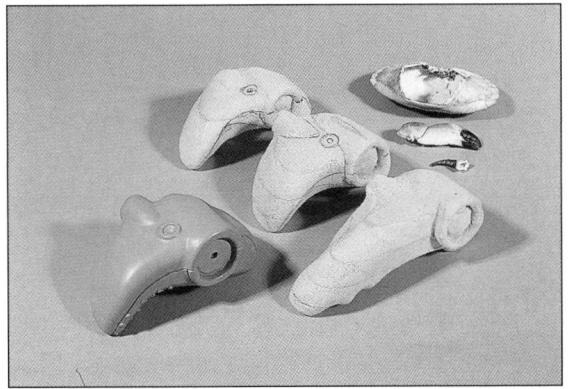

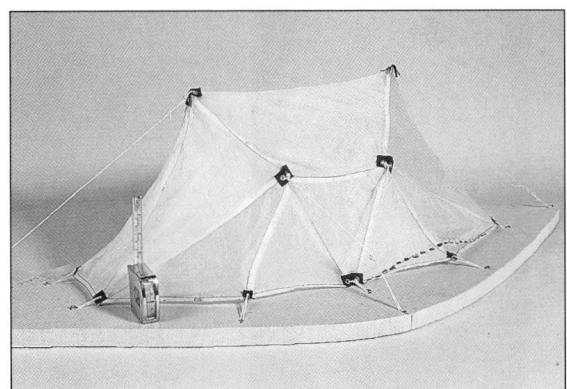

Exploring Materials

Creative and imaginative solutions to design problems can often be found simply by exploring the natural qualities of materials. For example, by experimenting with thin card you are likely to develop ideas for curving forms, whilst thicker card will probably lead to flat-sided structures. A good tip for developing initial ideas, therefore, is to explore a wide range of interesting materials. As a designer you should always be on the look out for new materials and for new ways of using them.

Card cut and stretched to make curves 2

Experiments in packaging using card 3

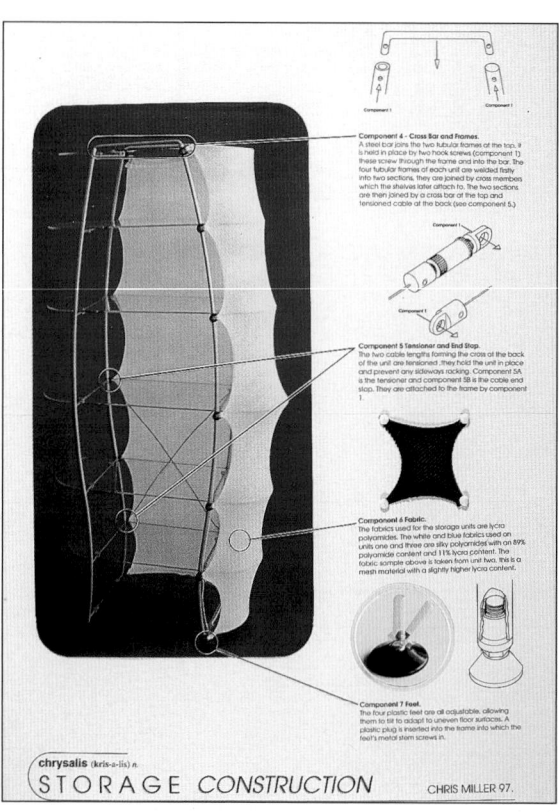
1

4

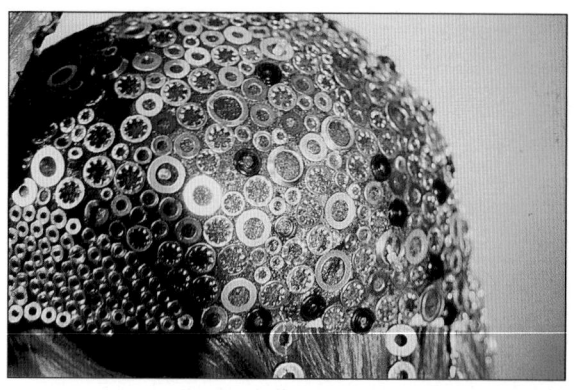
6

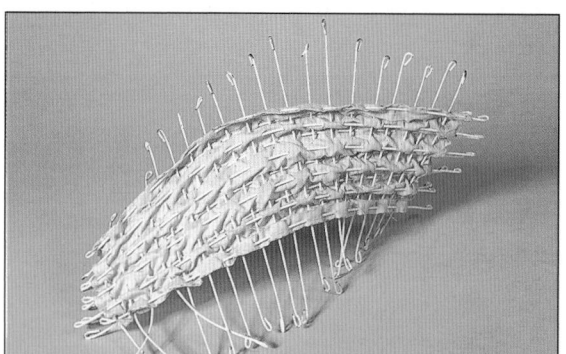
5

Fig. 1 Lycra stretched over steel wire

Fig. 4 Balloons filled and coated in silicone: inspiration for a lighting project

Fig. 5 Woven wire and fabric: early experiments for seating design

Fig. 6 Metal washers used to create interesting texture for a head-dress

Sheet materials such as paper, card and thin plastics are excellent for developing initial ideas. They are quick and easy to work and not too expensive to buy. Many useful materials of this type can be obtained by recycling used packaging. This source can also provide some of the more unusual forms of sheet materials such as mirrored card. By using very simple techniques such as cutting, scoring and folding you can easily explore both curved and rectangular forms. A few additional materials like string and wire will add further variety and allow you to extend the range of your initial idea development.

Product designers make quick appearance models in card by drawing details such as switches and dials onto the surface. Although these models are not completely accurate, they are very useful for getting an initial idea of what the product will look and feel like. Architects and interior designers also use this technique to produce simple scale models of buildings and interiors. Details like doors and windows are copied from the designer's drawings and pasted onto the walls.

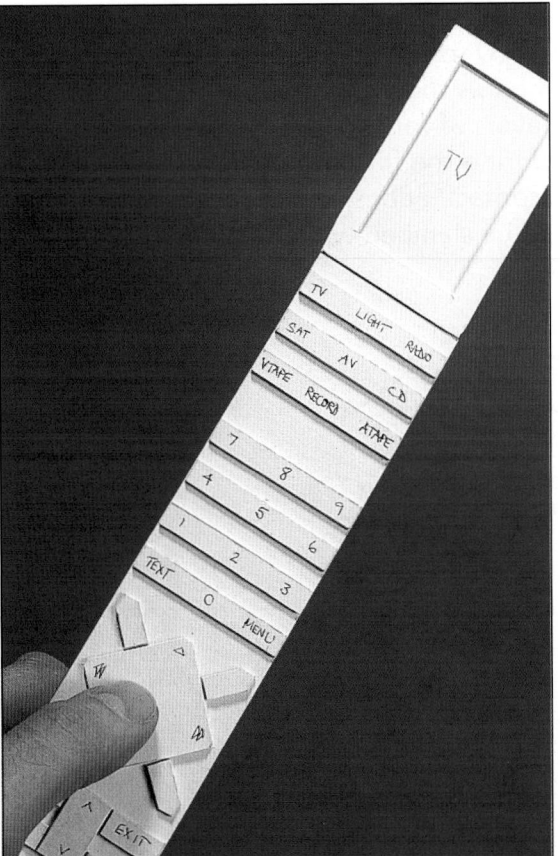

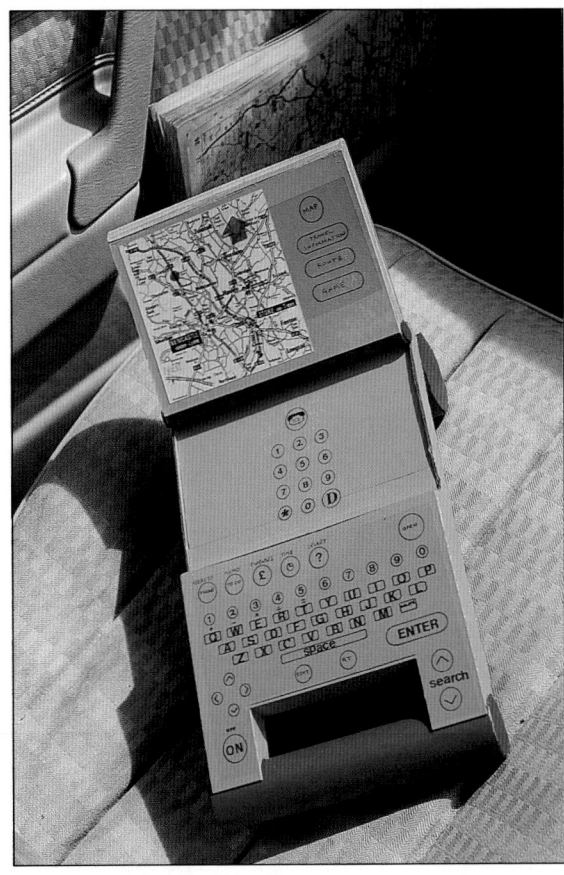

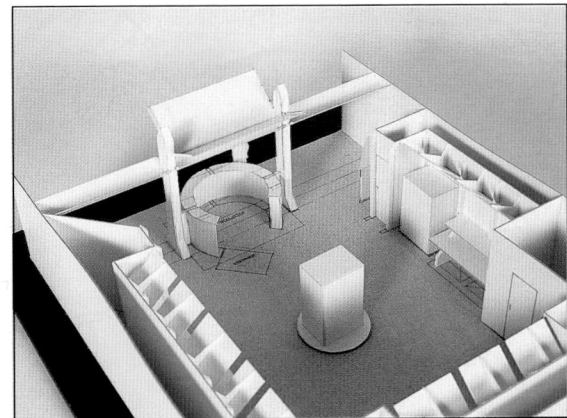

Laminating Card

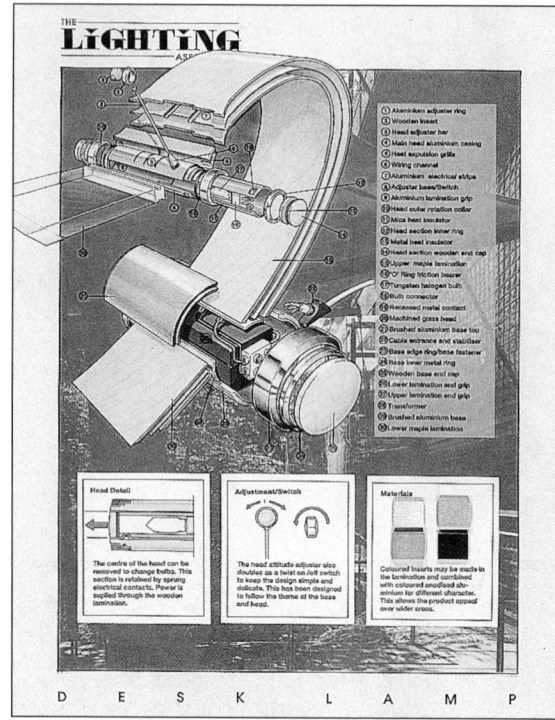

This technique is useful for modelling curved structures which need to be self-supporting.

- Cut enough pieces of card to make up the thickness.
- Use a glue stick to join them together.
- Before it sets, trim the edges with a craft knife.
- Use your fingers to form your design.
- Place it under a heavy object while the adhesive sets.

After about two hours, it will be rigid and ready to use. It is important to use a glue stick as this type of adhesive allows the layers of card to 'slip' across each other during the forming process. As it is also a 'contact' adhesive, the layers do not need to be clamped while setting.

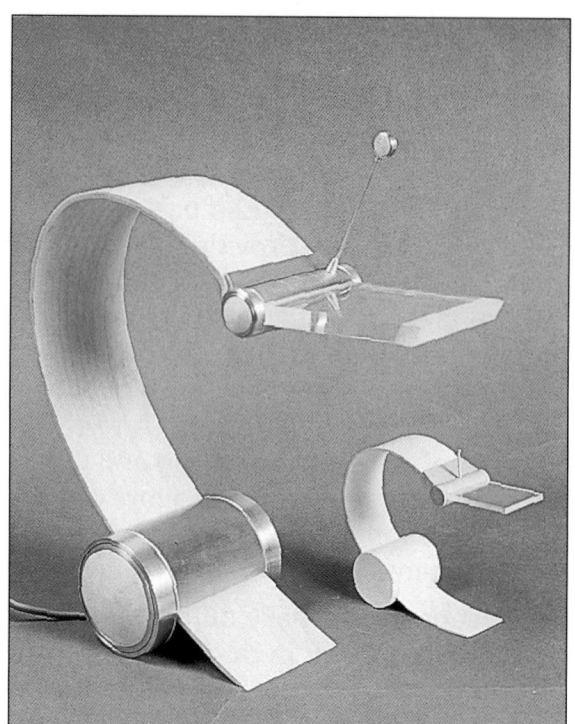

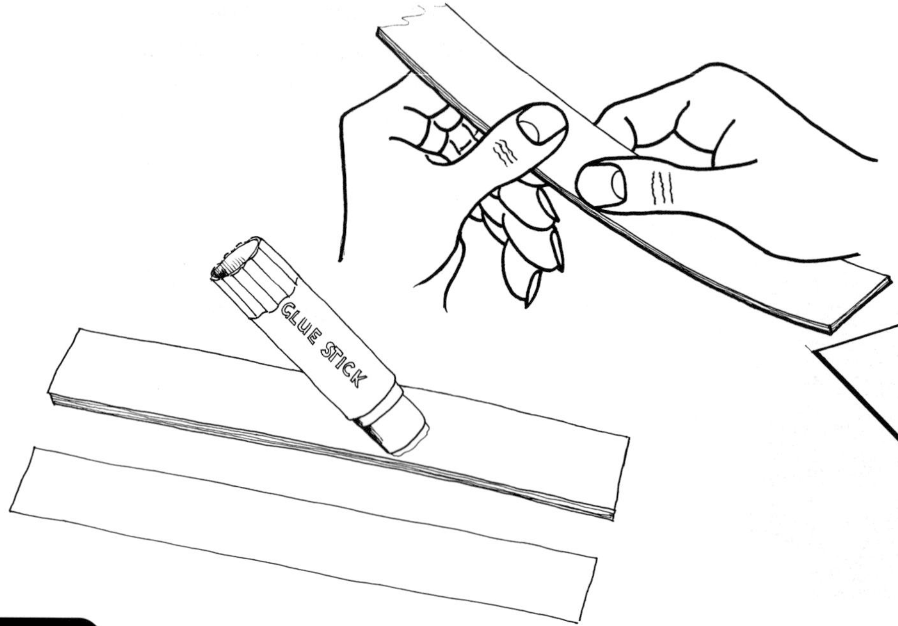

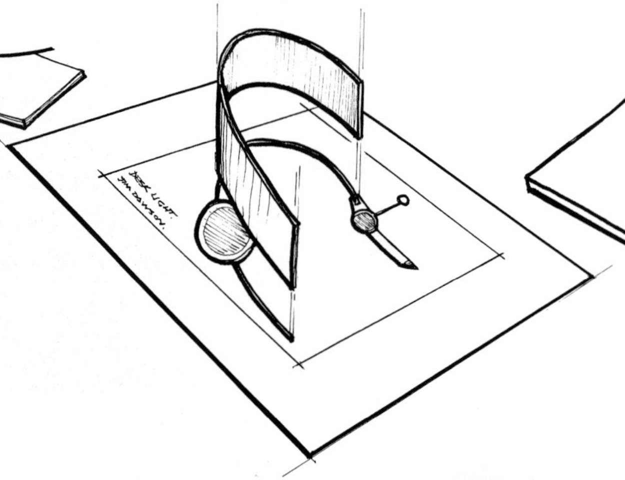

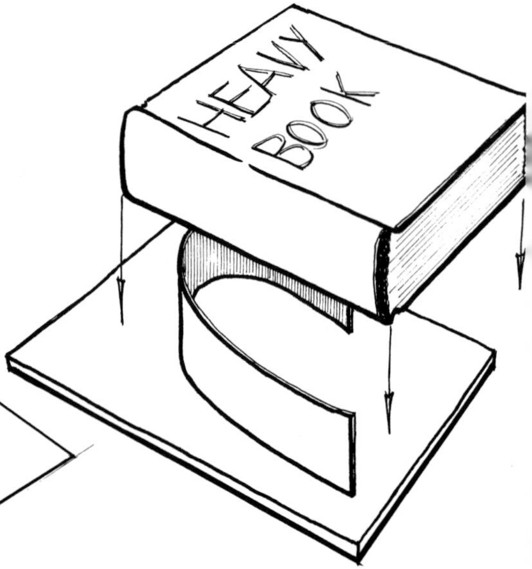

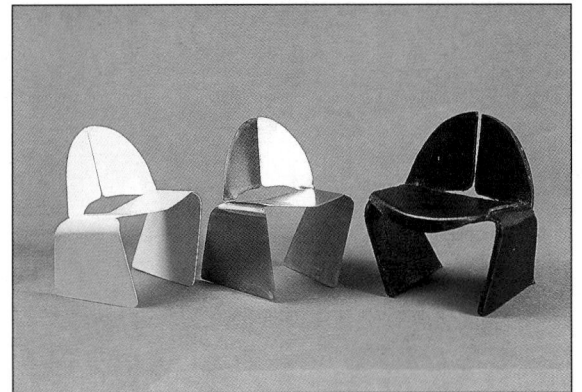

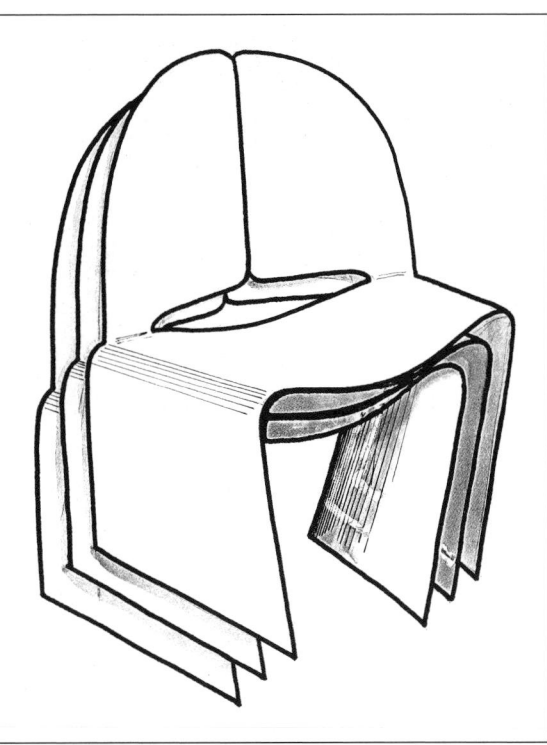

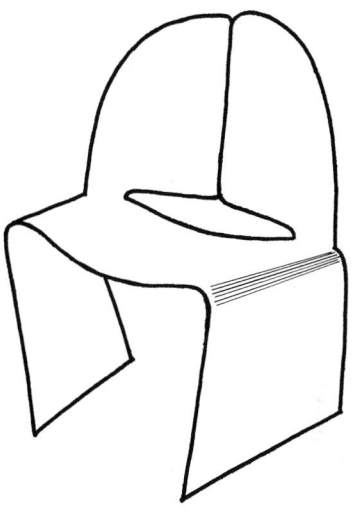

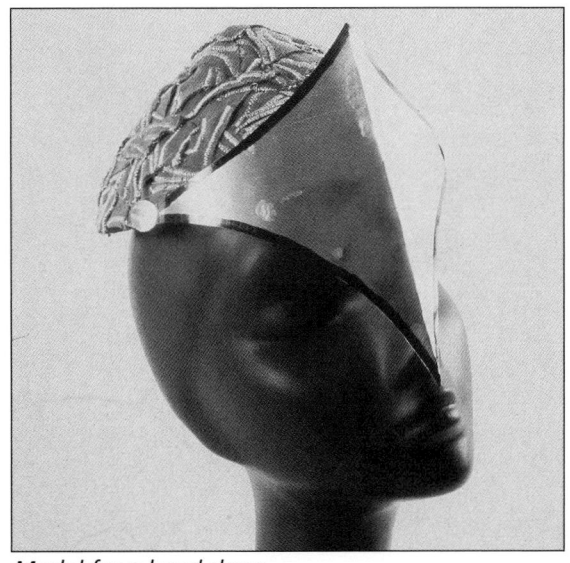

There are many useful materials that can be obtained from everyday objects. The designer who uses 3D modelling needs to keep an eye open for recycled materials and the possibilities that they offer. For example, you can obtain a flat sheet of thin, easily-worked material from an aluminium drinks can. As in this example, the net can be drawn on the sheet and then cut out with scissors. Folding, bending and rolling can then be used to create the three-dimensional form. This is easily done using simple hand methods.

NOTE: Take care with sharp edges.

Aluminium model for stacking chair

Model for a head-dress

Moulding Materials

Materials like clay and plasticine can be very useful for developing designs which involve curves in two and three dimensions. When you are designing this type of product, it is really important to build a physical model as you need to **feel** the form in order to fully appreciate and assess its quality. This **tactile** quality of products is very important. We have a natural instinct to pick things up and play with them.

A coffee maker. Initial model in plasticine and styrofoam

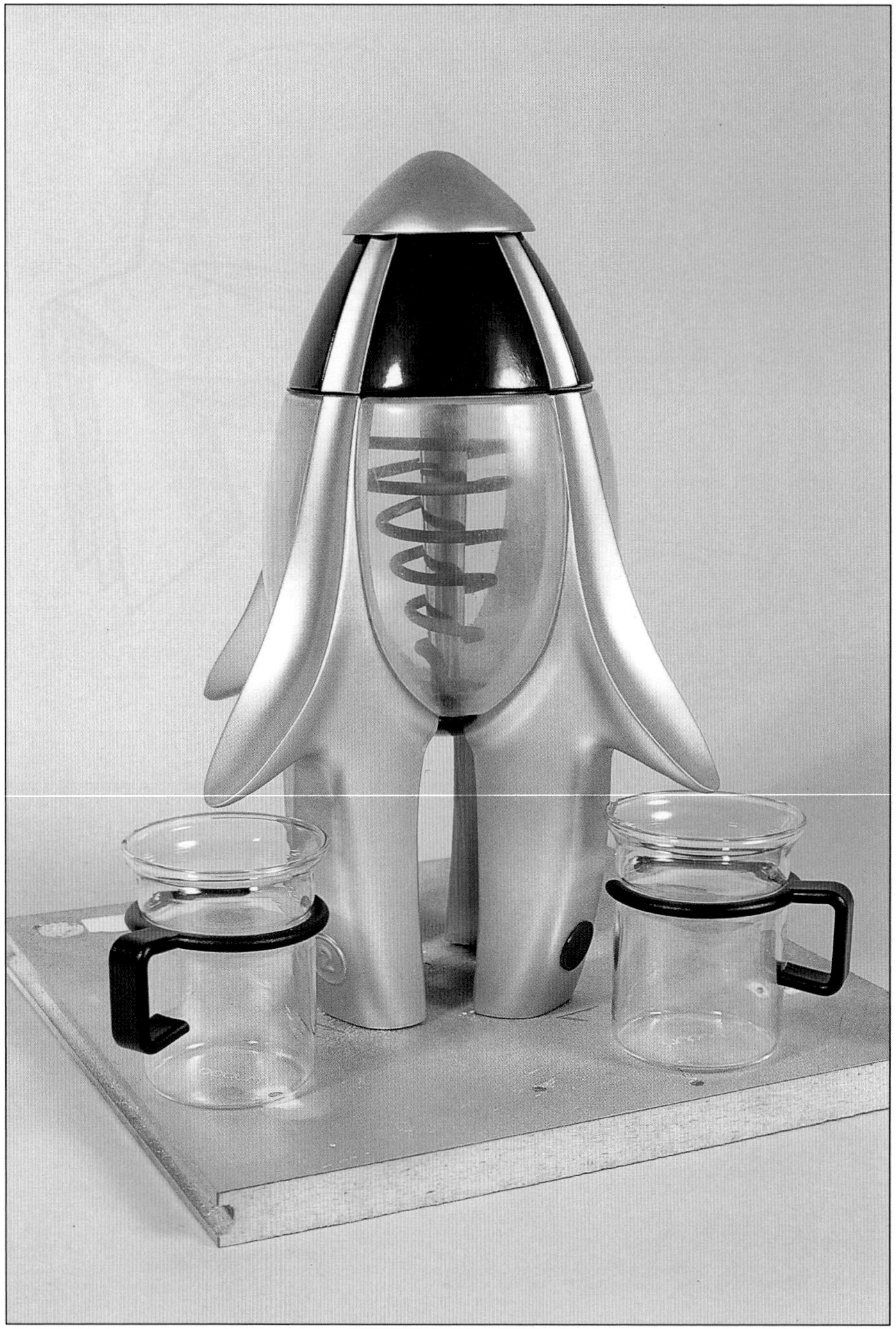

Final model cast in polyurethane resin

Clay is suitable for larger models, but if left uncovered it will dry out and become unworkable. To prevent this from happening you will need to cover it with polythene when you are not working on it. Plasticine is better for smaller models as it has the advantage of being reusable. Professional model-makers sometimes use a material called American Styling Wax. It is similar to plasticine, but has the further advantage of forming a hard surface which can be painted. For developing initial ideas, however, it is difficult to find a better material than plasticine. It is quick and easy to use and will allow you to pursue ideas almost as quickly as you can think of them. However, it is not a strong material and in thin sections it will not support its own weight without bending. To overcome this problem it may be necessary to build the plasticine onto a stiff wire core. By choosing a wire which is strong enough, and at the same time soft enough to bend by hand, you will create a composite material which will allow even more opportunities for your imagination to explore.

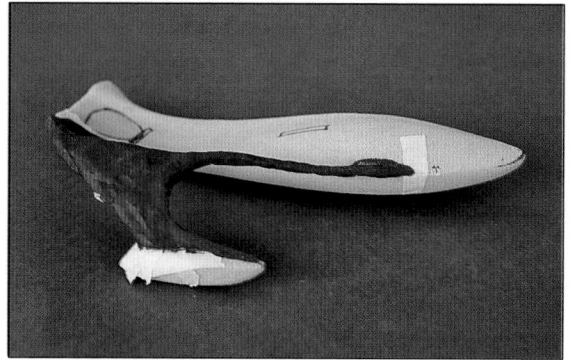

Early model of a trimaran in wire, styrofoam and plasticine

American Styling Wax on a wooden base

Finished model in wood and plastics

Block Models

Simple **block models** are very useful for developing the general feel and appearance of an object. For this reason they are frequently used in product and transport design where the forms involved can be complicated and therefore difficult to draw. They are also used by other designers when there is a need to establish the basic form of a design. For example, a furniture designer may well use block modelling to explore ideas for upholstered furniture.

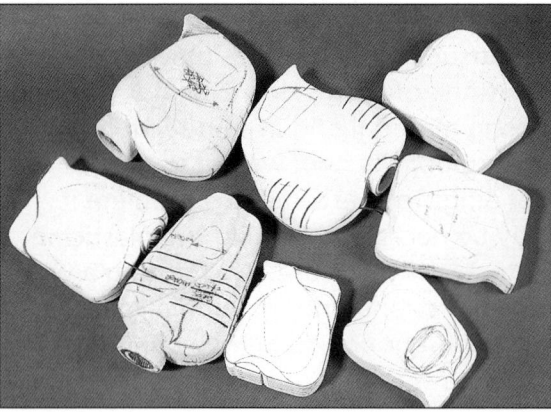

1

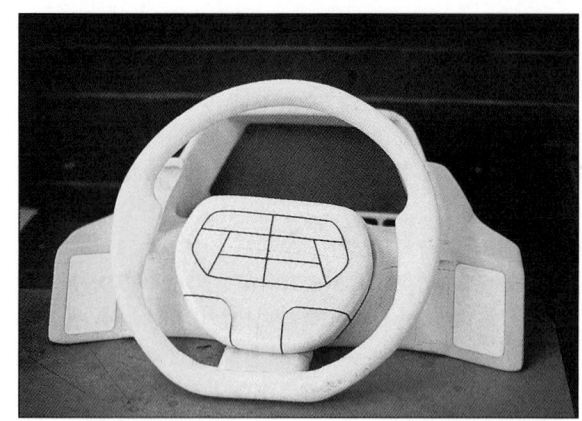

2

Polystyrene foam is a good material to use as it is cheap and easy to work. You can cut it with ordinary woodworking tools and much of the shaping can be done with sandpaper. There is a professional model-making grade, but the blue insulation grade works perfectly well for initial ideas. Other materials such as wood and MDF can be used, but these are harder and consequently more effort is needed to achieve a similar result.

NOTE: Always use foam in a well-ventilated area.

3

Fig. 1 Initial ideas for a digital camera

Fig. 2 Styrofoam steering wheel model

Fig. 3 Initial ideas for chairs, modelled in jelutong

There are two basic techniques for producing **block models**. In the first you simply carve away at a solid block of material until the desired form is achieved. In the second, pre-shaped blocks are glued together to create the required form. This latter technique is very useful as it allows you to produce recessed and internal surfaces without the need for expensive machine tools.

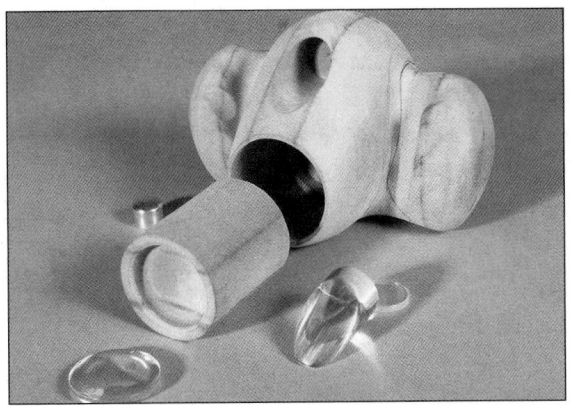

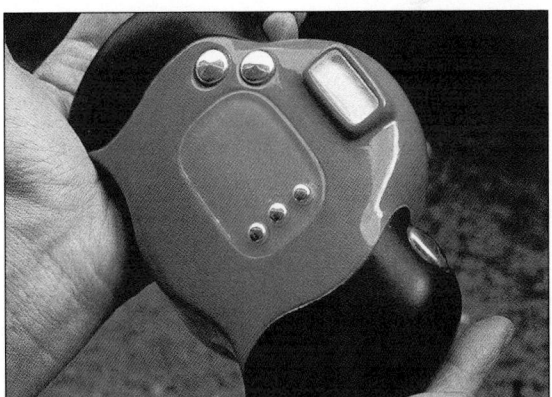

Frame Models

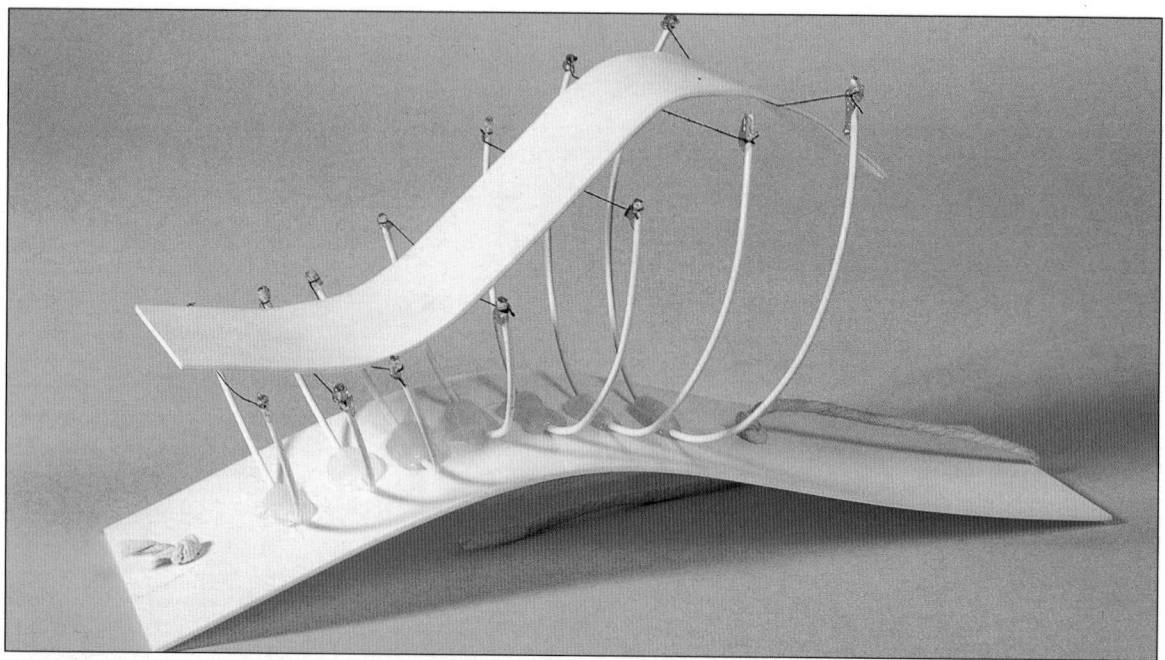

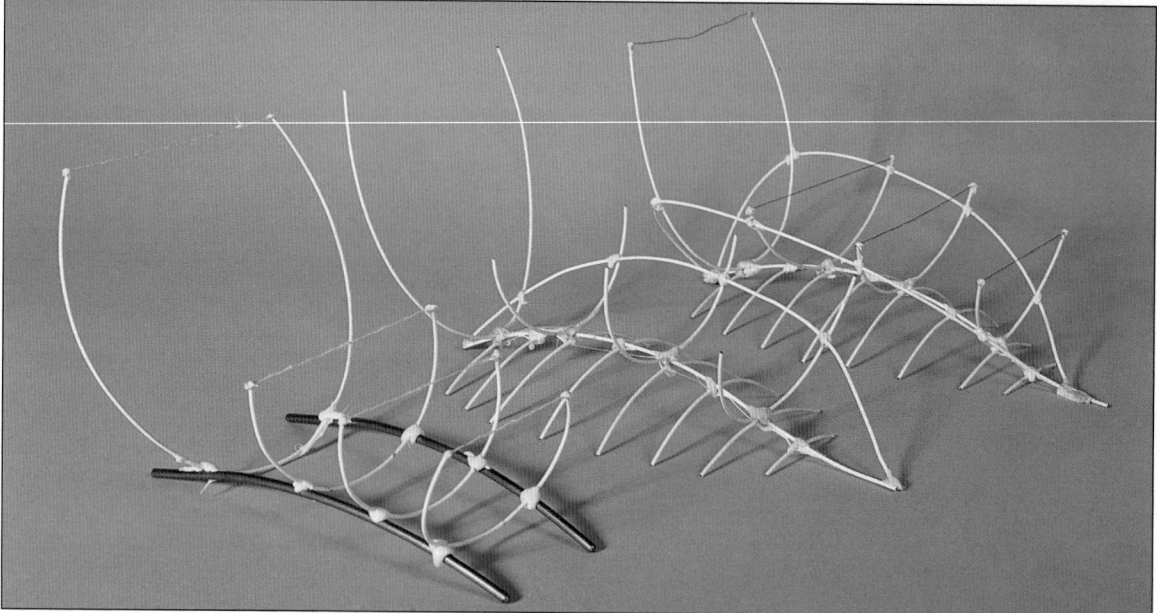

Early ideas for sunlounger

Frame models are normally built to scale and are used to explore and test structures. For example, if you intended to develop a new bicycle frame, you would probably need to build a series of models, first to develop your ideas, and then to test them. The choice of materials to develop initial ideas is not really important. Anything which is easily available, and which you can cut and join together without too much difficulty will suffice. Drinking straws, strips of wood, uncooked spaghetti and wire are all useful for this type of model. At this stage your intention should be to explore as many ideas as possible without worrying too much about how the structure will perform when used. Later models will need to be built from more carefully selected materials in order to test how the structure will react under working conditions. If the full-size structure is to be built from welded steel, then the model would probably be built from steel rods with soldered joints. Architects and engineers often build this type of model to test their designs. Because they need to be very accurate, such models are usually built by professional model makers.

Model-making kits were originally produced as toys. They have always had a serious intent, however, and the first of these, *Meccano*, is probably responsible for inspiring the current generation of professional engineers and designers. *Meccano*, along with *LEGO* and *LEGO TECHNIC* are examples of 'structural' kits. As the name suggests, they are very useful for exploring and developing structures. Bridges, buildings and vehicle chassis can all be produced from these kits. They are also useful for developing solutions to mechanical problems. *LEGO TECHNIC*, with its excellent range of gear wheels and mechanical components, is particularly useful in this respect. If you need to design a mechanism such as a mechanical grab then you will probably find one of these kits invaluable.

Using Kits

1

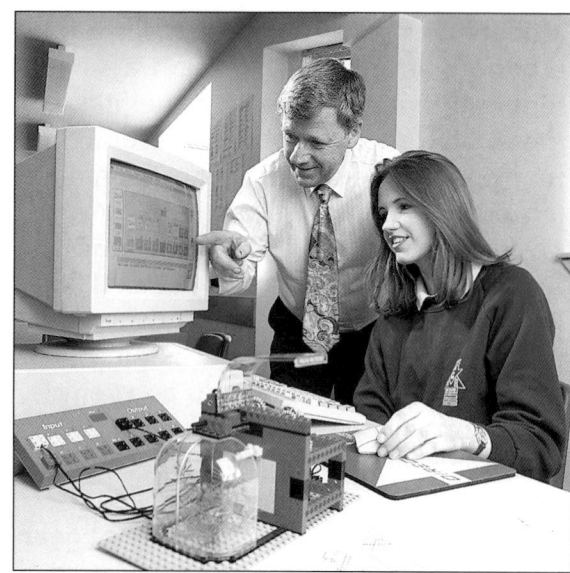

2

Fig. 1 Testing a differential gear mechanism

Fig. 2 A computer–controlled plant propagator

Fig. 3 Springboard electronics kit

Playing and designing are very similar activities. As designers we play with ideas. Subsequently, we test and evaluate them to develop the most successful way of doing something. Kits, whether electronic, pneumatic, hydraulic or structural, allow us to resolve certain problems more quickly than we could without them.

By using electronic kits we can build and test circuits without the trouble of soldering together numerous components. Similarly, pneumatic and hydraulic kits allow us to explore other aspects of power and control. They allow us to develop initial ideas without the need to build permanent, time-consuming models.

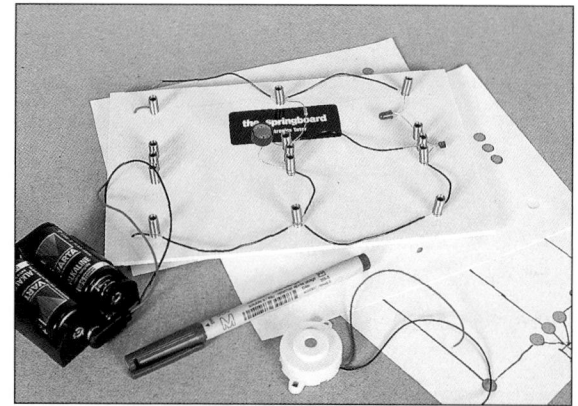

3

The use of information technology has made the life of the designer much easier in the way they can now model their ideas.

A simple method of using the computer to create an impression of a model is to use software that will 'extrude' a 2D image. This can be done in either one point or two point perspective. It is a quick method of producing simple forms which are symmetrical in one of the three dimensions. Depth of extrusion can be set to make the image look proportionally correct.

For those who find it difficult to generate freehand perspective drawings, this is a useful method of creating a three-dimensional image. The same principles apply in terms of setting the perspective to view more of one side than the other.

In a similar way, a two-dimensional drawing can be rotated around a given axis to simulate a 'turned' component produced on a lathe.

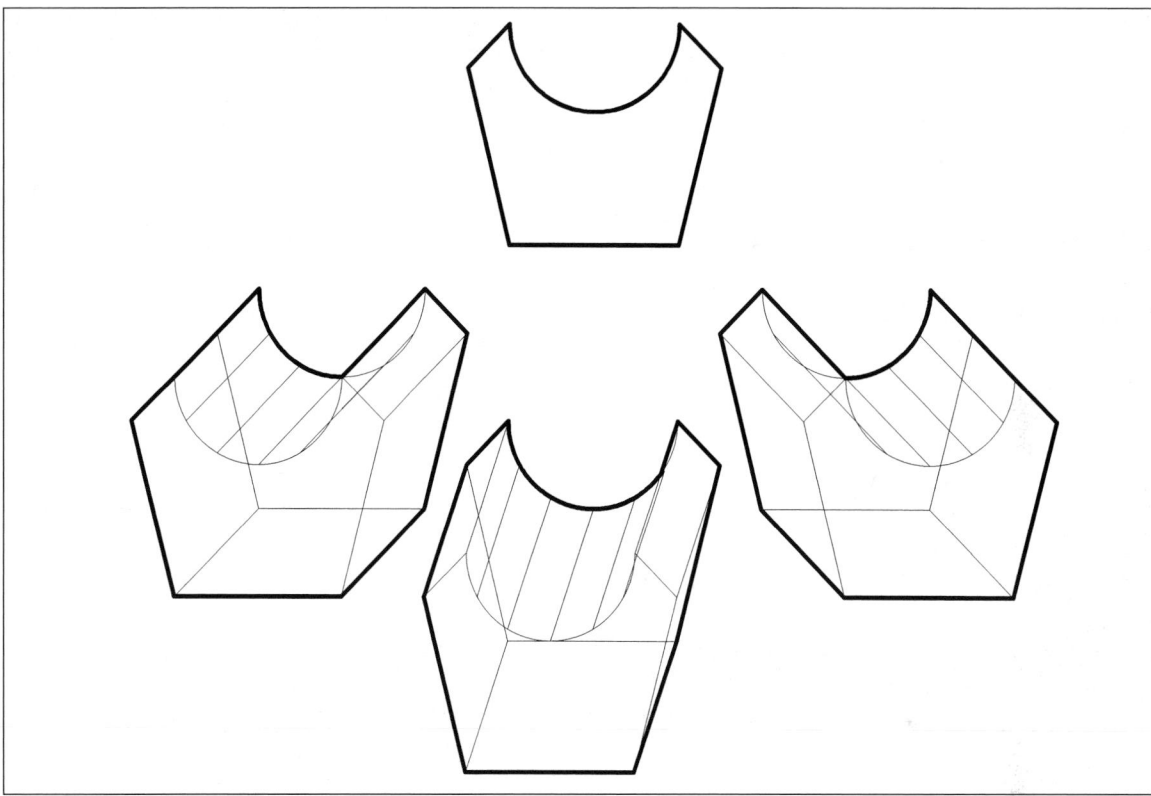

Range of 'extrusions' from the same 2D profile

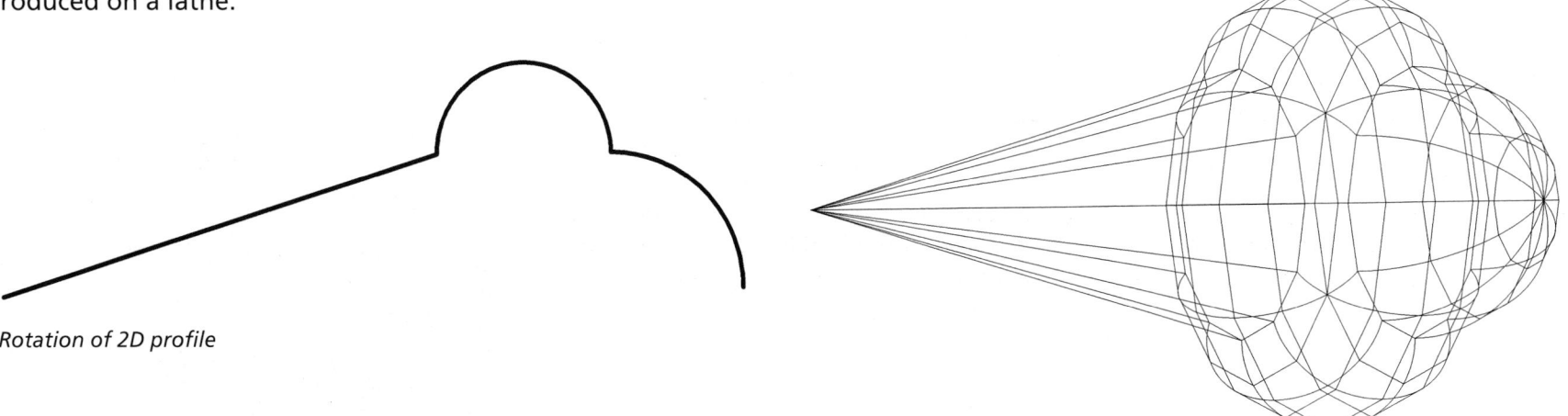

Rotation of 2D profile

2D CAD

Some of the simplest draw and paint software packages can be used to create geometric and freehand shapes which can then be coloured to give an impression of the finished thing.

In two-dimensional work, the individual components that go together to create a product can be drawn on screen and then manipulated to establish the correct proportions and sizes until the designer feels that they are correct. Once these have been produced, colour can be applied to give a more realistic impression of the product.

Colour variation and change of proportion can be done rapidly and many times over so that the designer can clearly establish what the computer model might look like in reality.

Textile pattern showing various colourways

Perfume bottle: variation in proportion

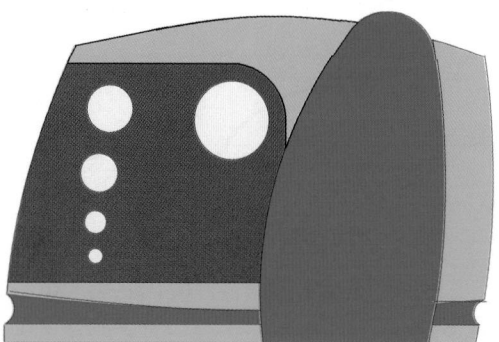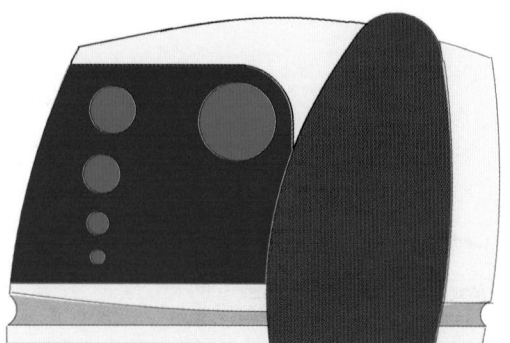

Toaster showing colour variation

This type of computer modelling is particularly good for the design of packages where the 'net' of a container can be drawn on screen. Text and graphics can then be added to simulate the two-dimensional surfaces of the finished object. Once these have been applied, they can be changed in a number of ways:

- Different lettering styles can be used.
- Different colours can be applied.
- Text and graphics can be moved around until the right 'look' is achieved.
- The size of individual parts can be varied to make certain features more prominent.

Text/colour variation

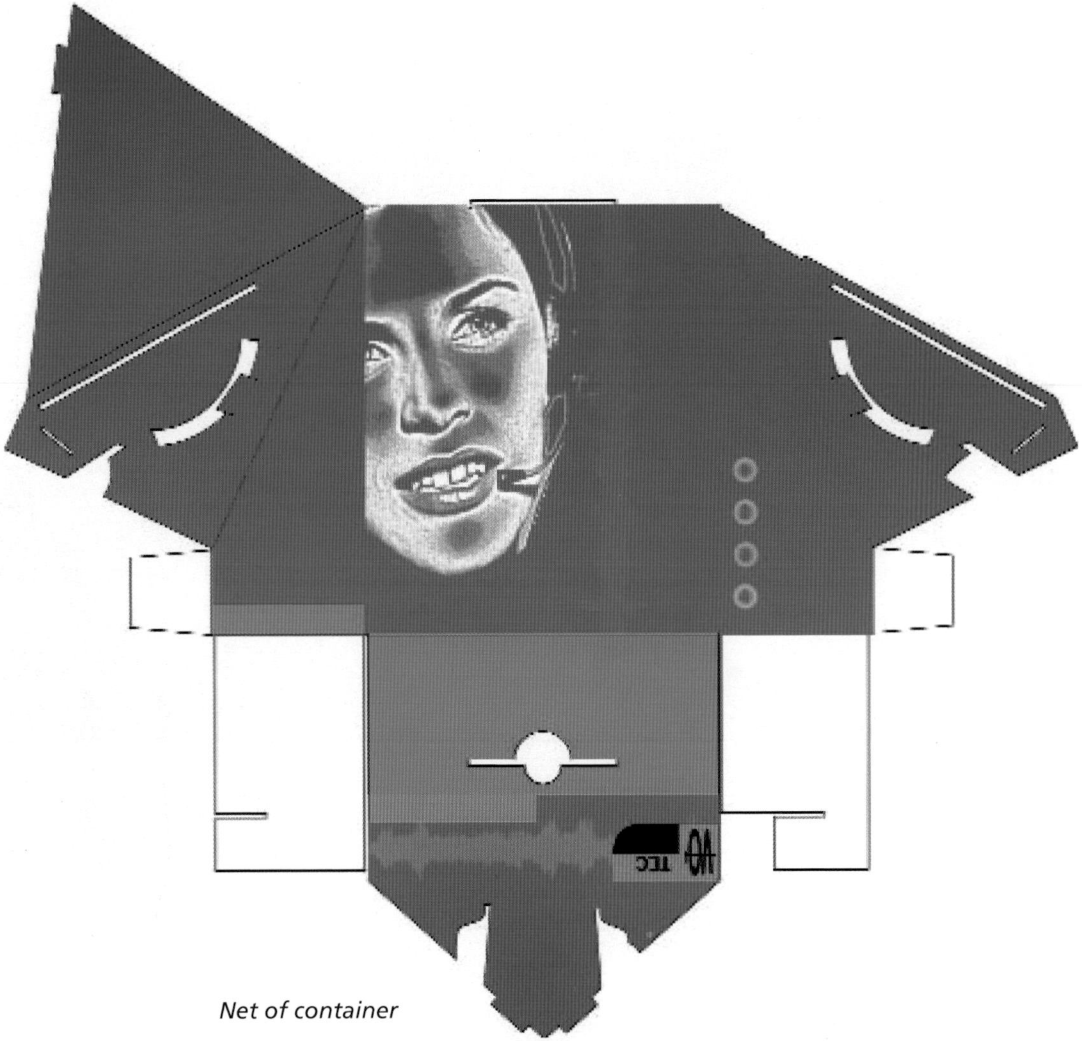

Finished package

Net of container

Developing Ideas

At some point in the design process you will need to take one of your initial ideas and develop it into a finished design. This is called **design development**. Your initial ideas will probably be in the form of sketches or sketch models and a lot of detail will be missing. The development stage involves filling in all the missing information. You will need to carefully consider all aspects of the design, such as the most suitable materials and most effective use of colour. You will need to ask lots of questions and then develop answers to all of them. The following pages explain this process in more detail and will help you to develop designs successfully.

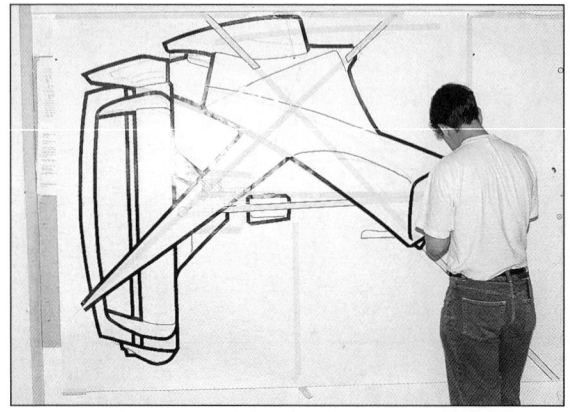

At the early stages of a design you will have produced sketches giving some idea of its appearance. In order to develop the idea further, you will need to make more considered decisions about the forms that you intend to use. Sketches, measured drawings and computer models are all useful in helping to develop form, but where detailed choices need to be made, there is no substitute for a carefully made model (this is particularly true where the forms involved are complicated). In some cases it is necessary to make a series of models of the same design so that you can compare one idea with another. Even small changes to one visual element within a design can have a dramatic effect. The chief advantage of using models is that you can *feel* as well as *see* the quality of the form.

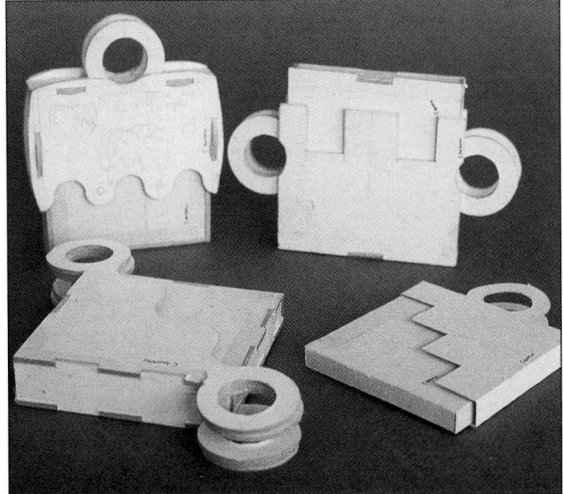

Size and Proportion

When designing any new object you will need to decide exactly what size it needs to be. This is not simply a question of how big the product needs to be in order to do its job. It is also a question of choosing a size that looks right. It is all too easy to design a chair which functions well, but which just looks too big and clumsy. To avoid making this kind of mistake, it is a good idea to make a full-size model.

Making visual judgements on models seen in workshops can often result in products which appear to be too big when they are placed in a normal domestic interior. Full-size models really need to be seen in the kind of space where they will eventually be used. As their main function is to give an impression of size, they need not be fully detailed. In fact, in order to consider size, a model of a chair could be made

from pieces of wood and cardboard held together with masking tape. It is helpful, however, if all the parts are of the same colour. Colour can affect how big an object appears to be – light colours can make something appear larger than it really is. Therefore, if parts of a model are different colours, making visual judgements about size is made more complex.

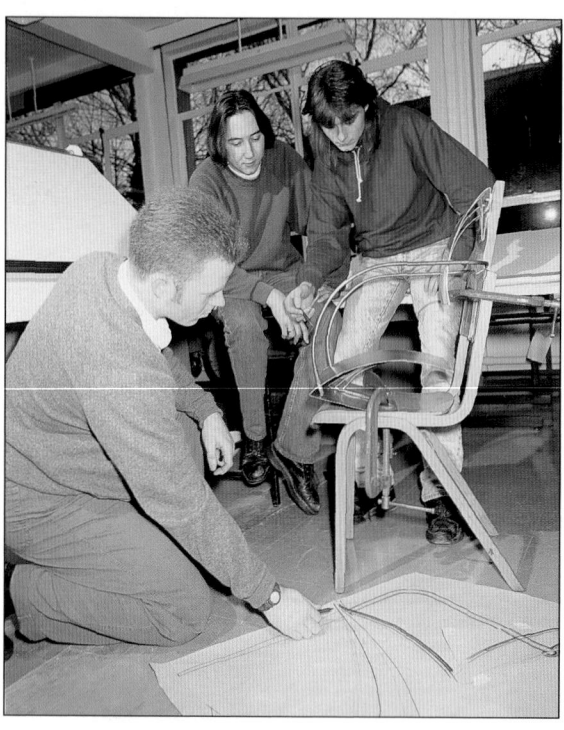

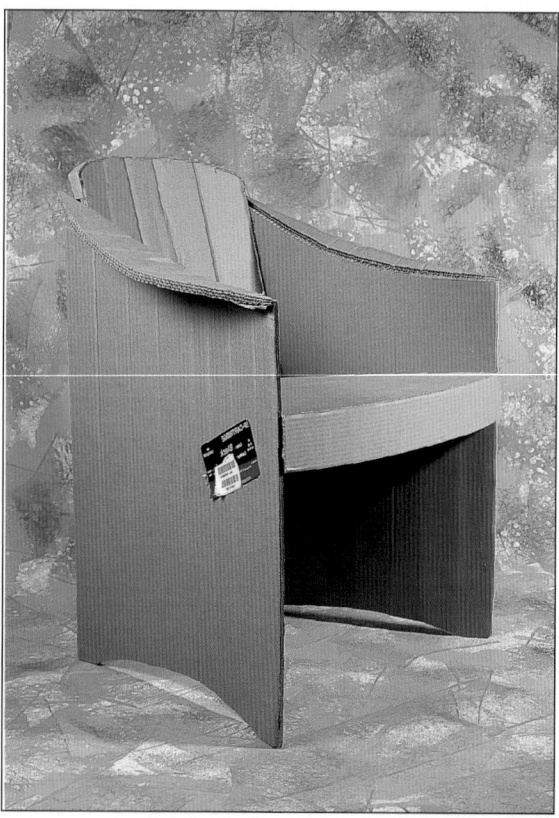

Full-size model of a chair made from scrap card

Painted model: allows the designer to make judgements about proportion

As well as making decisions about the overall size, you also need to think about the size of the component parts. To some extent this can be achieved by using measured drawings. Obviously some of the dimensions will be fixed by physical requirements, such as the height of a seat, though finer judgements will be concerned with aesthetics rather than function. Good proportions can be achieved by balancing the size of one component with another, rather like deciding on the layout of a 2D design. When working in 3D it is easier to make these judgements by using models so that the full effect of three dimensions can be considered.

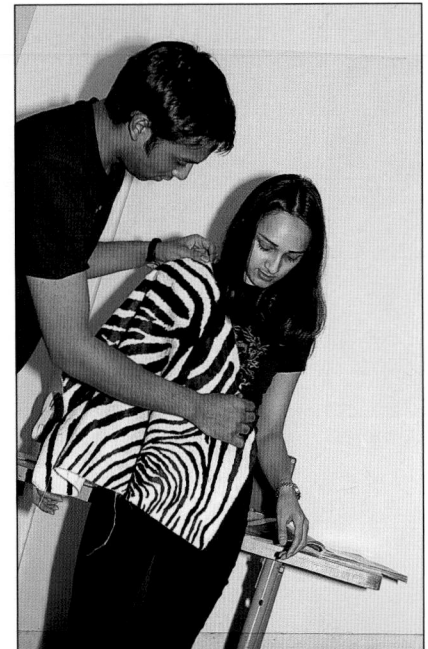

Small-scale models are not as useful when making decisions about size and proportion. This is because the visual balance between parts of the design can change when it is made full size. Decisions which you may have been happy with at small scale, suddenly look wrong when seen at full size. This is less of a problem with larger products such as buildings and interiors which we normally view from a distance. Consequently, architects usually develop their ideas through scale models, whilst clothes designers prefer to model at full size.

Developing the proportions of a hi-fi speaker

Texture

Texture is very important in design. A suitable texture can enliven an otherwise ordinary product. It must be applied with sensitivity and restraint, otherwise the overall effect can look chaotic. Interior designers collect samples to compare the wide range of materials which they often use. It is essential for the designer to feel and handle textures in order to appreciate their tactile qualities and to decide which are appropriate in a particular situation.

Rather than relying on small samples, product designers prefer to apply texture directly to their models. In this way, it is possible to see what the effect will be (and feel like) on the finished design.

Textures can make a model appear realistic and believable or, if not treated carefully, they can very easily have the reverse effect. In interior design, textures and patterns must be scaled down to suit the scale of the model or the effect will look clumsy and amateurish. For example, it is better to use a coarse-textured paper to represent carpet as this will be more suited to the reduced scale of the model.

Interior design with fabric samples

This small-scale model with carefully selected materials gives a realistic effect. The figure is cut from a magazine and pasted onto card

It is possible to create textural effects by applying real materials to models. For example fine wire mesh can be used to represent speaker grills on radios and other audio equipment. In other cases, however, this may not be possible and you will need to be inventive and resourceful in order to give the impression of the material in the final product.

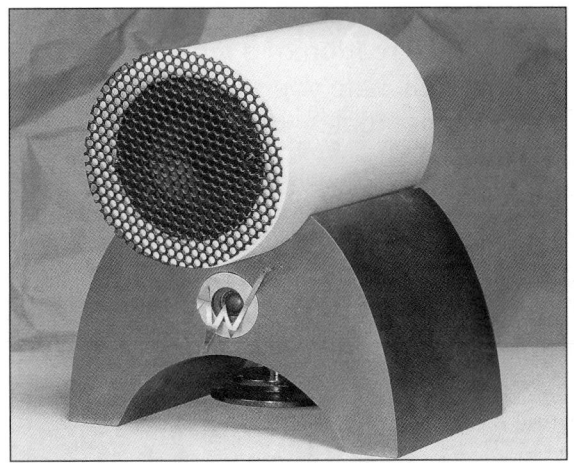

Wire mesh speaker grill

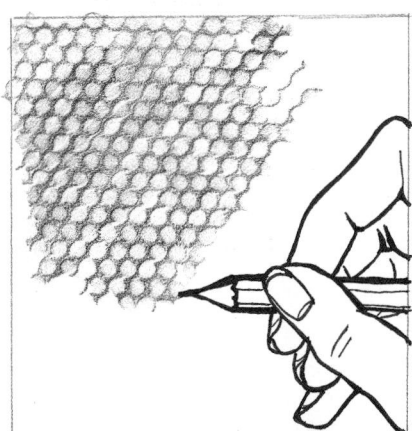

Pencil rubbing over perforated sheet

You can show texture in a drawing by copying the effects of light and shade on an object. For example, to represent a gloss finish you can create the sharp highlights of the shiny surface by using strongly contrasting light and dark tones in a drawing medium that gives smooth colour (pastels or markers). A rough texture such as mesh for the speaker grill, can be produced by placing paper over the wire mesh and rubbing lightly with a pencil. This can then be reduced on a photocopier to fit the scale of the drawing.

If you make several photocopies of the outline of your design drawing you can easily experiment with different textures and gain an idea of the visual effect of different surface finishes and materials.

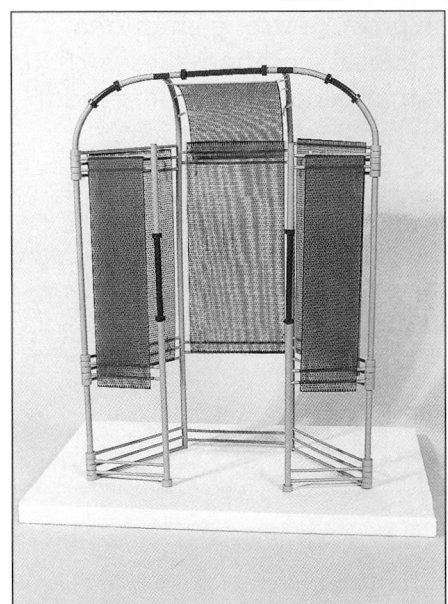

Dry transfer mesh on acetate

Contrasts of light and shade used to produce a metallic effect

Colour

Choosing colours for your design can be exciting, but there is more to finding an effective colour scheme than just using the ones that appeal to you the most.

When we look at an object it is usually the colour that is the first thing to strike us. It can instantly attract our attention and convey strong messages about the quality of the object. For example, we have come to associate pastel pinks and powder blues with delicate and gentle items such as cosmetics or baby products. These delicate colours would seem 'wrong' used in the design of an electric drill or the packaging of batteries as we associate these products with power and energy.

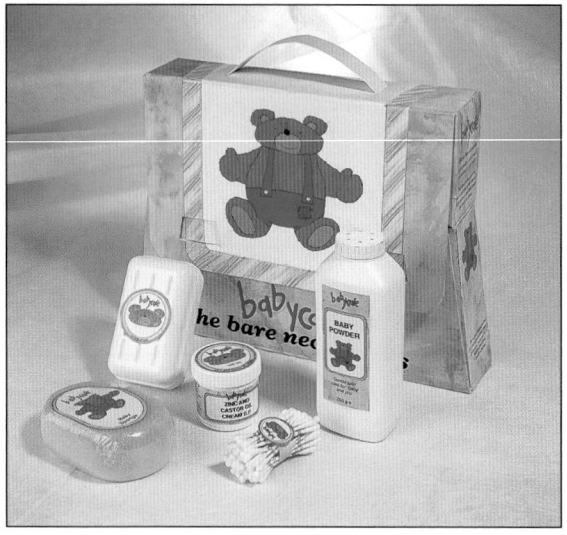

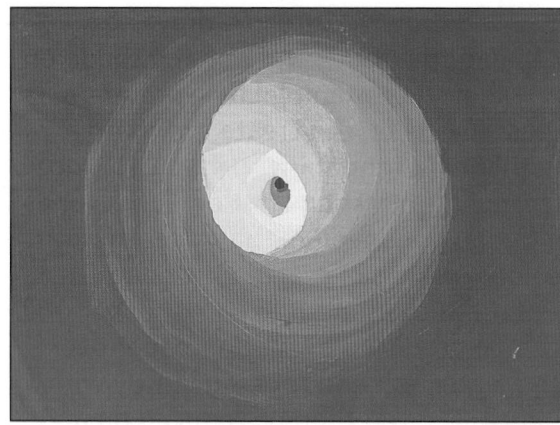

Some of our responses to colour may be simply through association – reds and oranges seem warm like fire; blues are cool like ice or the sea; browns may suggest a natural quality because we connect them with the colour of earth, wood or leather. At a deeper level, colours can provoke strong emotional and even physical sensations. Research has shown that people sitting in a room with strong red lighting soon feel irritable and uncomfortable and that their blood pressure may even rise.

When selecting a colour for a design, you must decide exactly what **message** your design will communicate.

It is useful to write a list of words that describe the identity of your design:

Modern Exciting Unusual Fun	Reliable Traditional Strong Masculine	Exotic Romantic Expensive Mysterious

Each of these groups of words communicates a very different type of image. The creation of a mood board (see page 11) will help you select colours and patterns that match your list.

When you feel that you are close to finding an ideal colour scheme, it is important to actually try it out. Use a colouring method that is quick in conjunction with either a computer image or photocopies of your design. Experiment with different tones of the chosen colour and try unusual combinations of colour.

You will discover that you can completely change the nature of a colour by positioning it next to another that may contrast. For example, blues can be calm and peaceful but used next to a hot orange, they will create a more jazzy mood.

Before applying colour to your final design it is helpful to test out your colour scheme at full size, if possible. You may be surprised at the effect produced by a large area of colour; it will look quite different from a small sample swatch. If you colour a simple card model or even a sheet of paper, you will be able to judge the changes in colour that light and shade make to a form. These effects will vary depending on whether the finish is gloss, matt or textured.

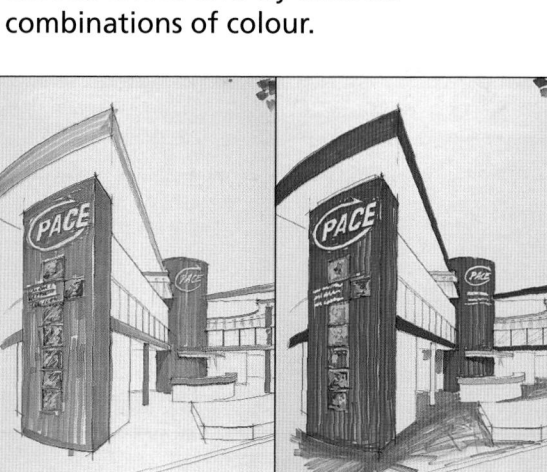

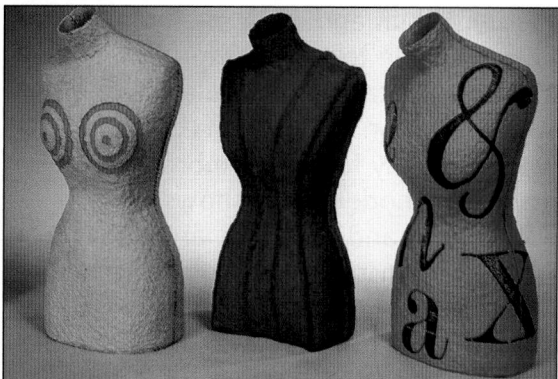

Different colour effects on papier maché clothes stand

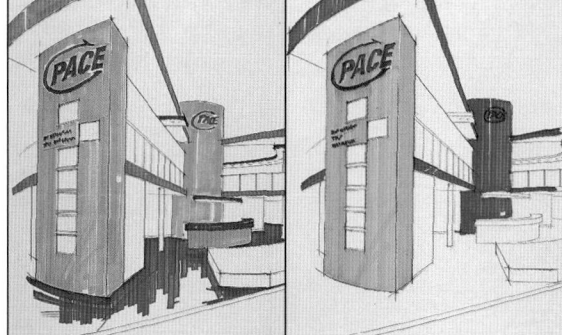

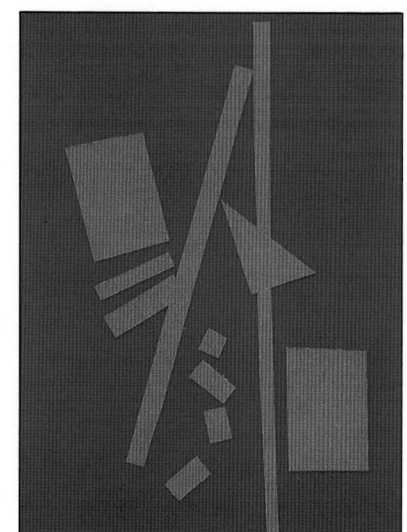

Colour scheme for an exhibition stand

The use of colour-test models will allow you to make personal decisions as well as to seek the opinion of others. Its application will help you to decide if the tone or shade is right, if colour combinations are effective or if the colour of small contrasting details need adjusting.

Test Models

When developing an idea, you will probably need to make different types of model to test different parts of the design. For example, the design of a folding chair will probably need a full-size model to test its structure, as well as other models to test details such as the folding mechanism. Some of these models are easier to make than others.

As a designer you shouldn't expect to be able to make everything you design. Fully-working models or **prototypes** are often very complex and need the specialist skills and equipment which are only available to manufacturers. Mechanisms can be particularly difficult. So, rather than trying to make a chair which actually folds, it is more sensible to make one model which shows the appearance and structure, and another which demonstrates how it will work. In this way you can model your ideas for the mechanism separately, and use materials which are easier to work than those needed in the model that you sit on.

2

1

Fig. 1
Appearance model of a car security system designed to clamp onto the control pedals

Fig. 2 & 3
Test model to explore the mechanisim and ergonomics

3

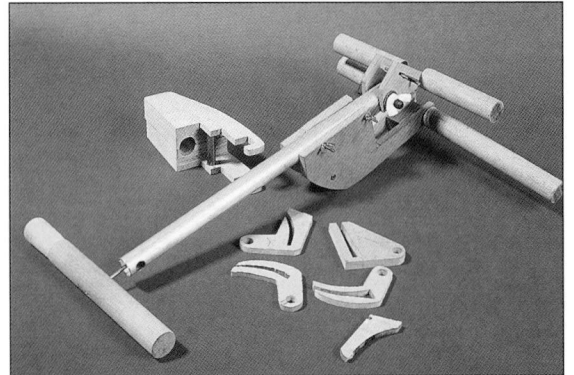

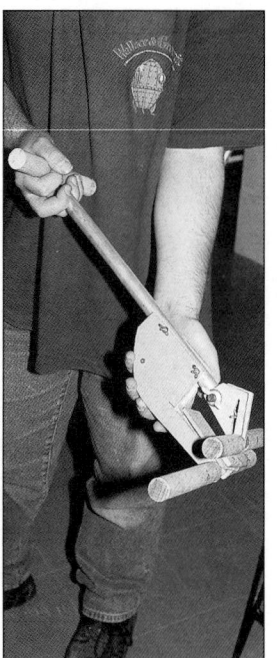

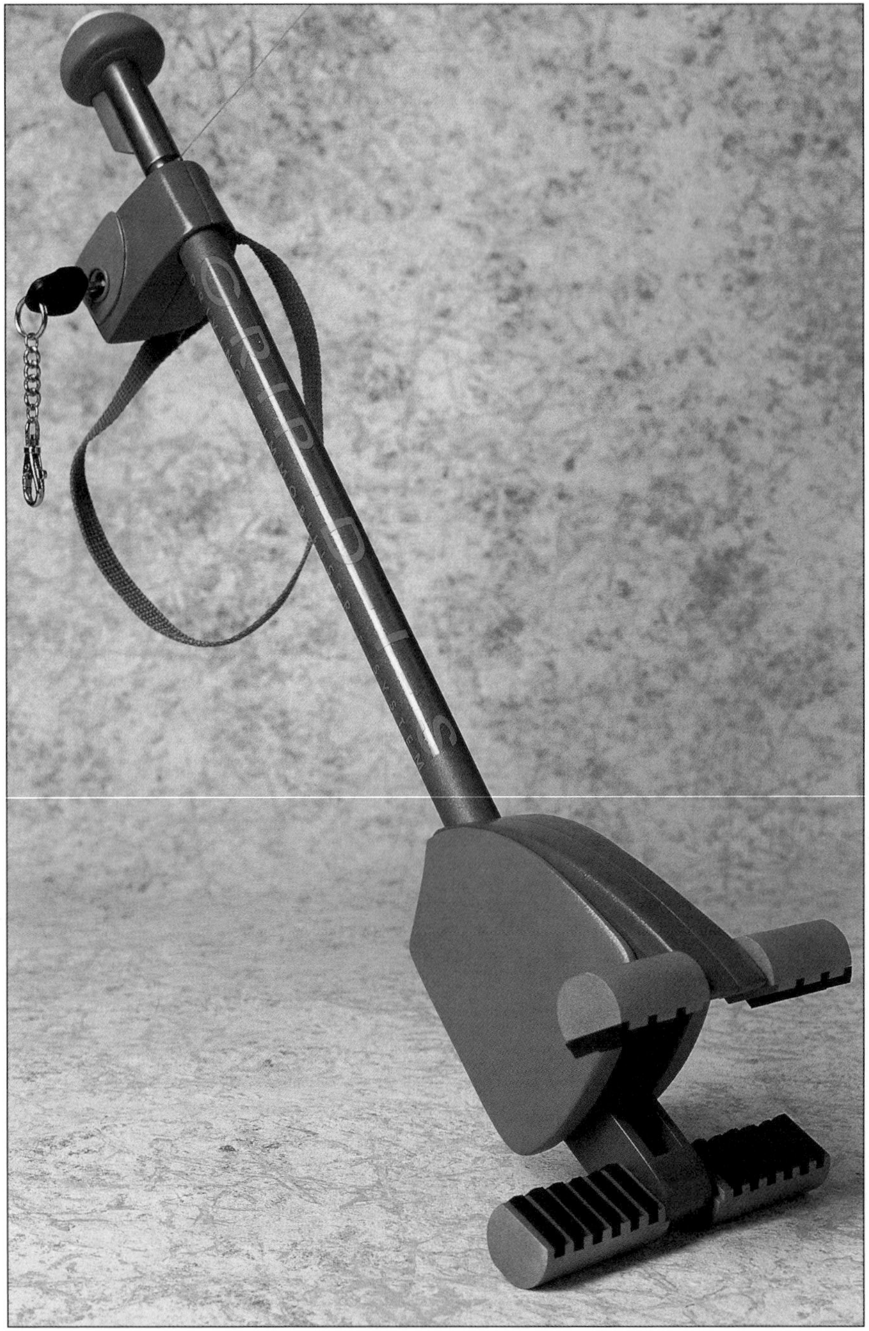

Because of the need for change and adaptability, test models are sometimes built from kits. The ease with which components can be removed or replaced make these systems useful for developing designs where there is a mechanical, structural or control problem. In other cases, any method which allows materials to be temporarily joined together is helpful. This kind of model will test your ingenuity. You will need to be resourceful and inventive. Adhesive tape and paper clips work with lighter materials, but you may need to use 'G' cramps, or something similar, for bigger models.

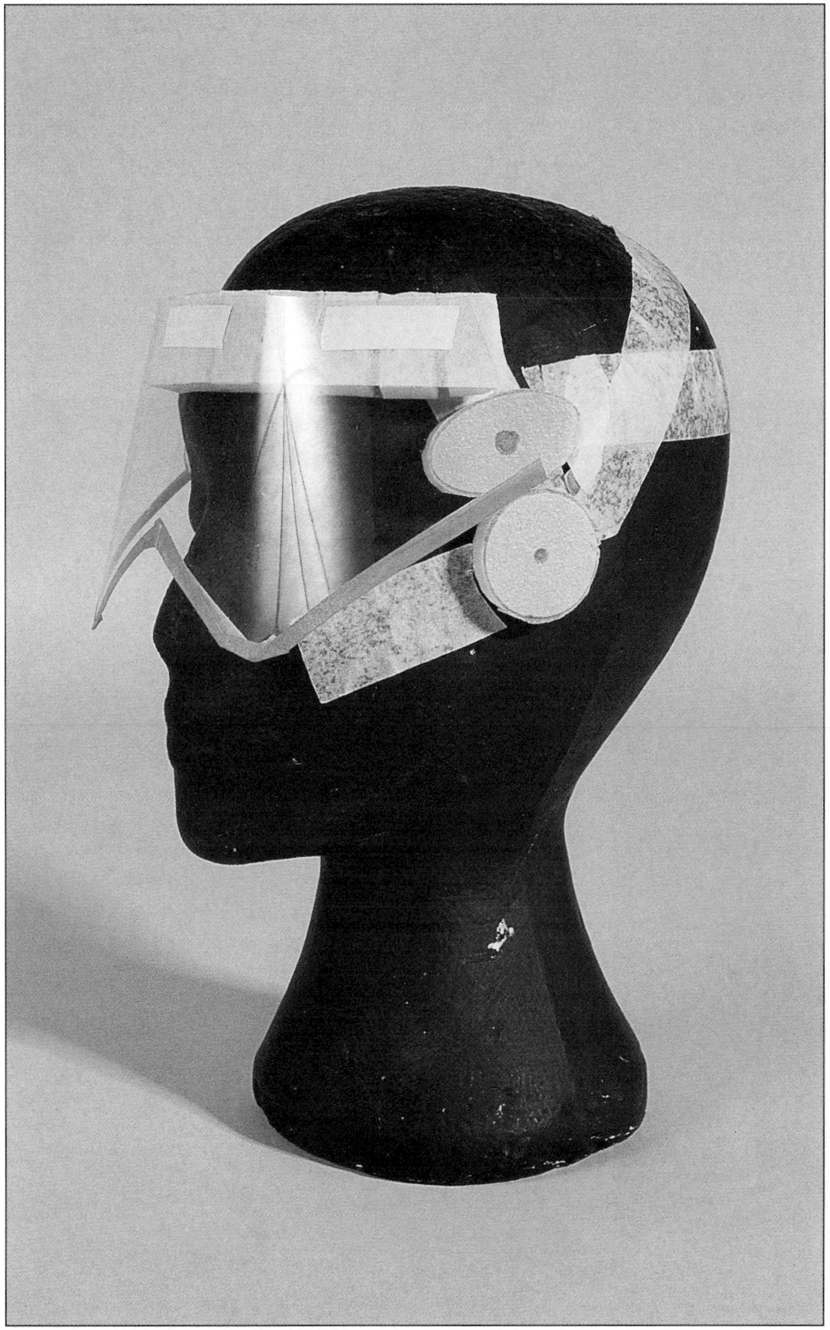

Early lash-up for workshop safety visor

Test Models / Performance

When developing ideas for a design, you may need to explore the ways in which it might work. For example, the brief for a mood light may state that it should create a dramatic effect within a room. The only way to know whether your ideas will achieve this effect is to experiment with different light sources and with a range of materials to shade, diffuse or to reflect the light.

Because you are gradually building your ideas, models of this type need to be adaptable and not permanently fixed together. As a result, the term **'lash-up'** is sometimes applied, as such models are often tied together with string, wire, masking tape, or any other device which can be quickly removed to enable the design to be altered.

In other situations, performance models may need to be made more carefully. A good example of this is the models used by architects to test their design proposals against the effects of high winds and earthquakes. In order for these tests to be of any real value, such models need to be made accurately, with similar physical qualities to their full-sized equivalents.

1

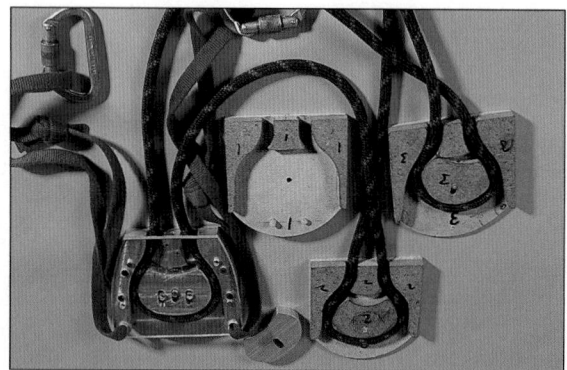

2

NOTE: Of course, where electricity is involved, the usual safety procedures should be followed, and the circuit must be safety tested before it is switched on.

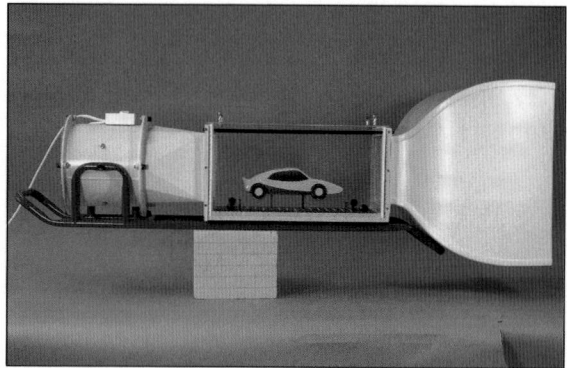

3

Fig. 1 Light casting dramatic shadows

Fig. 2 Lash-ups for a rope control system for climbers

Fig. 3 Testing aerodynamics of a car design

Many products rely on systems in order to make them work. Think of the series of events which makes a car go faster when the accelerator is pressed. There will be a mechanism which connects the pedal to the carburettor, where in turn a series of levers, valves and pipes deliver a measured amount of fuel into the engine. Systems like this are very complicated and almost impossible to resolve without development models.

A board game is another good example of a system design. A series of events is linked together to achieve an overall effect. The game can only be successful if the designer carefully works out how each event fits into the overall scheme. It is difficult to see how a game like *Monopoly* could have been developed without little blocks of wood, strips of paper and sheets of cardboard, as they enable the designer to test the relationships between all the parts of the design.

Test model for a board game

Test Models / Ergonomics

Ergonomics helps us to develop products which are easy for people to use. A good example of this would be the design of a tractor cab. A driver spends many hours every day working in this small space. It is, therefore, very important that the design of the seat and the layout of the controls are carefully developed in order to make the work as easy as possible. The design of such complex products has been made very much easier by the use of computer models. They enable the designer to experiment with the position of the component parts in relation to the user without needing to build full-sized models.

In some situations, however, designers prefer to work with physical models. They give an immediate and more easily understood impression of size and physical relationships. This type of model need not be expensive or difficult to make. Furniture and product designers often build full-size models from cheap materials such as corrugated card in order to test the ergonomic content of their design proposals.

4

1

2

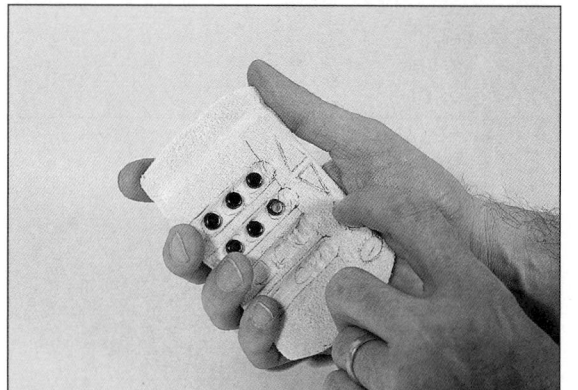

3

Fig. 2 *Early model for a power skateboard*

Fig. 3 *Testing the layout and size of a remote control*

Fig. 4 *Testing the design of a trike*

In two-dimensional modelling, small details on a drawing can be difficult to see and understand. To make these clearer, an enlarged view of such details can be added to the drawing to show the observer what is happening. This can be attached to the original drawing by placing a frame around it to emphasise the magnification. It will help to focus attention on the detail yet visually separate it from the overall view. If the frame is circular, it will give the impression of viewing the detail through a magnifying glass.

There are also occasions when the designer is working on designs that are so small that it is necessary to model them in a larger scale. These ideas for a range of tweezers would have been difficult to understand if they had been modelled to the actual size. By modelling them in a larger scale, both the overall form and the details can be understood more easily.

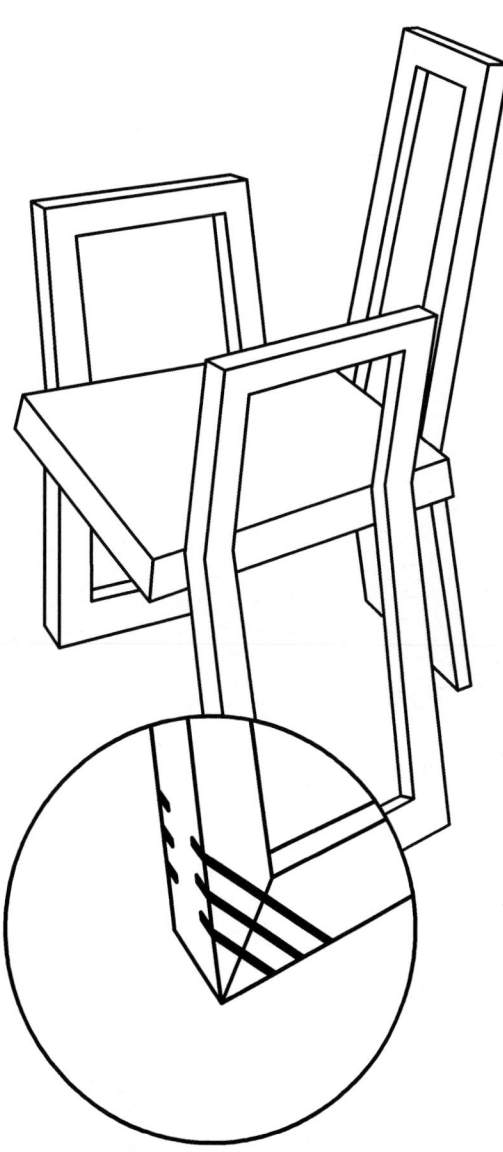

When modelling in three dimensions, there are times when it is necessary to work in a magnified scale to gain a better understanding of how the detail might work. Moving parts are a good example of this where it might be necessary to demonstrate how a particular feature will work.

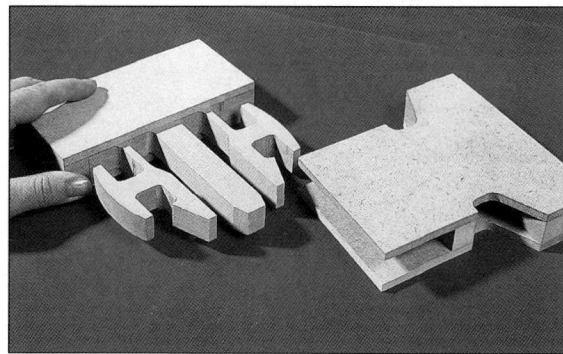

Enlarged detail of a ruck–sack clip

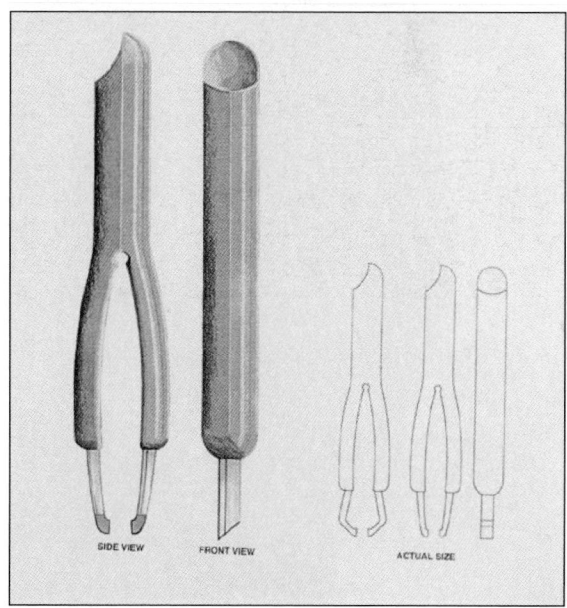

Context

The size, shape and quality of a space have a strong effect on the way we see the objects that are placed there. Consequently, during development, designs must be checked against the background where they will be seen and used. In many cases this is easy – you can ask someone to model a coat, or even to wear it in a particular kind of location – though with other products it may be more difficult.

A computer generated image of the Millennium Dome in situ

Buildings are a good example. It is not really possible to try out a building in a particular location just to see what it will look like. One way in which architects get around this problem is to use photography. By drawing an image of the proposed building onto a photograph, it is possible to see what the new building will look like in its new setting. Computers have made this technique much easier, and some of the images produced in this way are very convincing indeed.

Proposed design for Millennium Tower

If it is not practical to put a full-size model into the location, you can create the illusion of this by using one of these techniques.

Here a small-scale model has been made to look life size. A photograph of the model was pasted onto the background garden scene. The man is posing as if he is holding the model in order to make the result more convincing.

The image above was produced by placing a small-scale model in front of a background photograph. A cut-out figure from a magazine was pasted onto card and placed behind the bench to give an idea of scale.

Useful tips:

- Use the camera at a low angle to create a realistic perspective.

- Sometimes photographing a small part of the model helps to give a more realistic impression of a full–sized product.

Orthographic Drawing

For each complete design, it will usually be necessary to produce an **orthographic** or **working** drawing. This should include all the necessary information for you, or someone else, to make the finished article. In order to include all the information, the three main sides are drawn as two-dimensional images – front view, side view and plan view. To draw these accurately, you should use the correct type of drawing equipment (tee square and set square).

The two types of orthographic drawing normally used are called **1st angle projection** and **3rd angle projection**. Each has its own symbol so that anyone reading the drawing will be able to understand which type it is.

1st angle is symbolised by

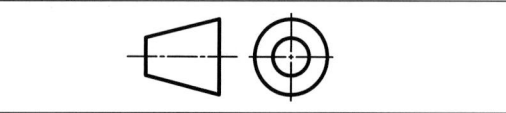

3rd angle is symbolised by

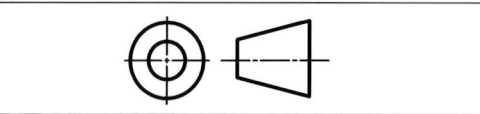

To explain the principles of both types of projection it is best to imagine the object being suspended in a box.

FIRST ANGLE PROJECTION

The object is suspended near the bottom right-hand corner of the box, being the same distance away from each surface. Imagine that the top, front and end views are then projected onto the three surfaces of the corner. In other words, what you see of the front view is drawn on the surface immediately behind the object.

When the box is unfolded, the three views can be seen next to each other in two-dimensional form. From this we can see that lines projected from one view will line up with those in any of the other two views. This is the basis for constructing the drawing. The end view is to the right of the front view and the plan is below it.

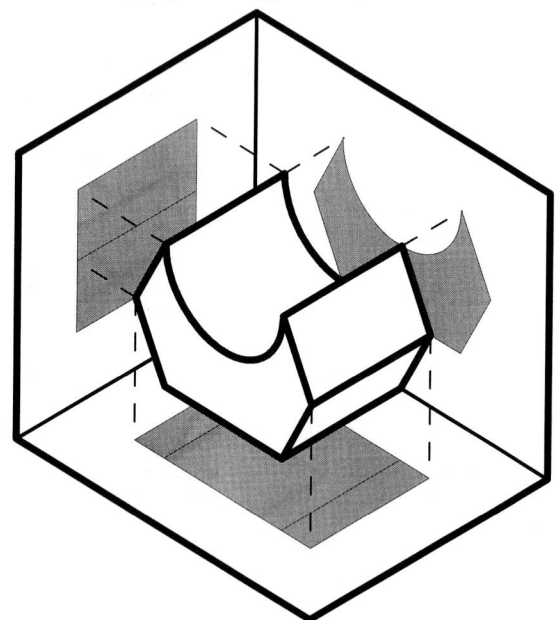

Object suspended in 'box' corner

Box being opened

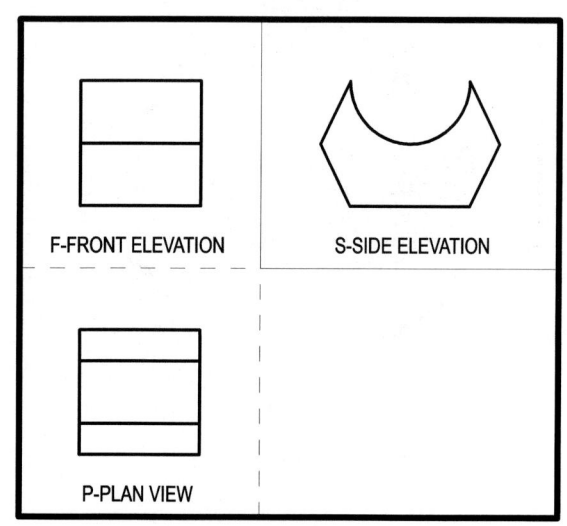

F-FRONT ELEVATION   S-SIDE ELEVATION

P-PLAN VIEW

Orthographic drawing of object

THIRD ANGLE PROJECTION

A similar method to first angle projection but this time the object is suspended in the top left-hand corner of the box. The three views are then projected back towards the three surfaces of the box.

Again, when the box is unfolded, the three views are seen next to each other but this time the plan is above the front view with the side view to the left of it.

The views that we see in both types of projection will, at this point, only show the visible edges of the object. It will be necessary to show those edges that cannot be seen or which are 'hidden' and this is done using a broken line.

Because an orthographic drawing is an accurate method of showing an object in two-dimensional form, it will need to contain all the necessary information about its size.

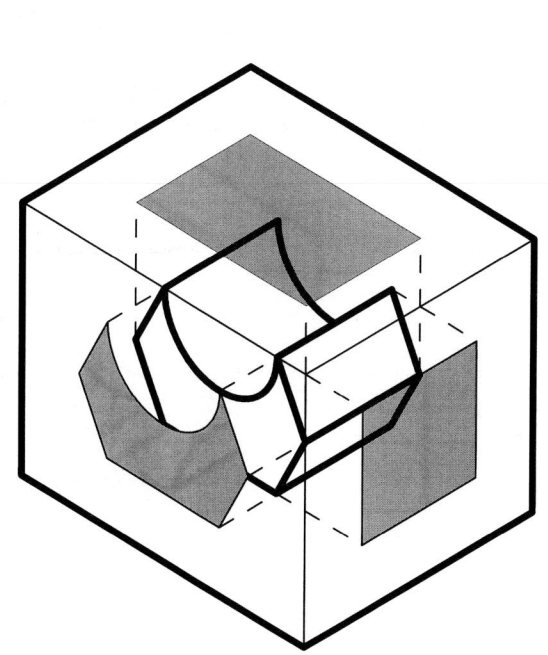

Object suspended in 'box' corner

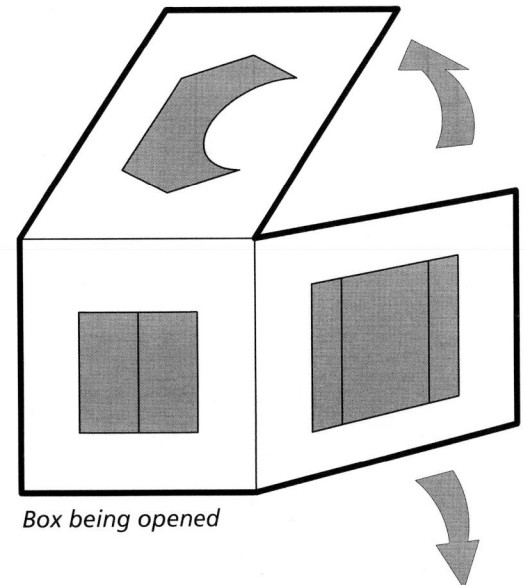

Box being opened

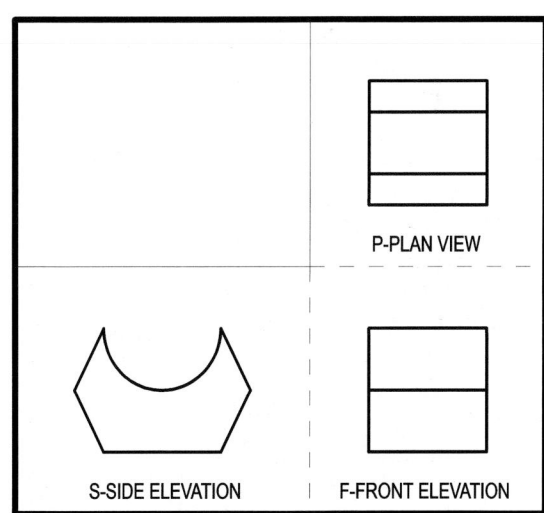

P-PLAN VIEW

S-SIDE ELEVATION   F-FRONT ELEVATION

Orthographic drawing of object

Orthographic Views

The benefit of orthographic drawing in developing ideas is that any one of the views can be used to consider the location of various types of detail such as switches, knobs, lettering, etc. Using one of these views is less complex than a perspective view, and it takes less time to produce. Many variations of detail can be tested by drawing the two-dimensional view, photocopying it and then trying out different layouts.

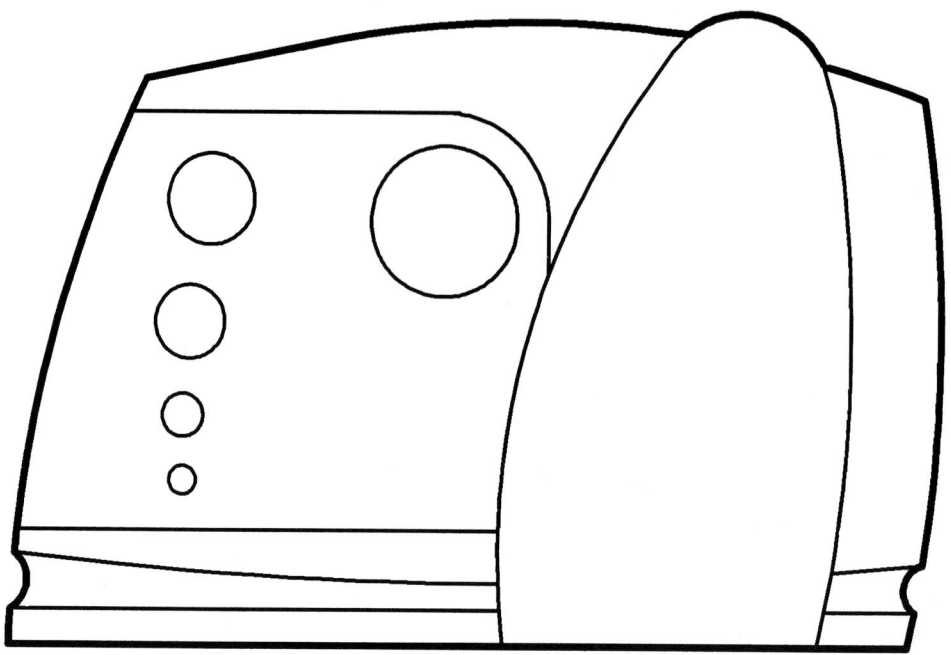

Basic form of toaster

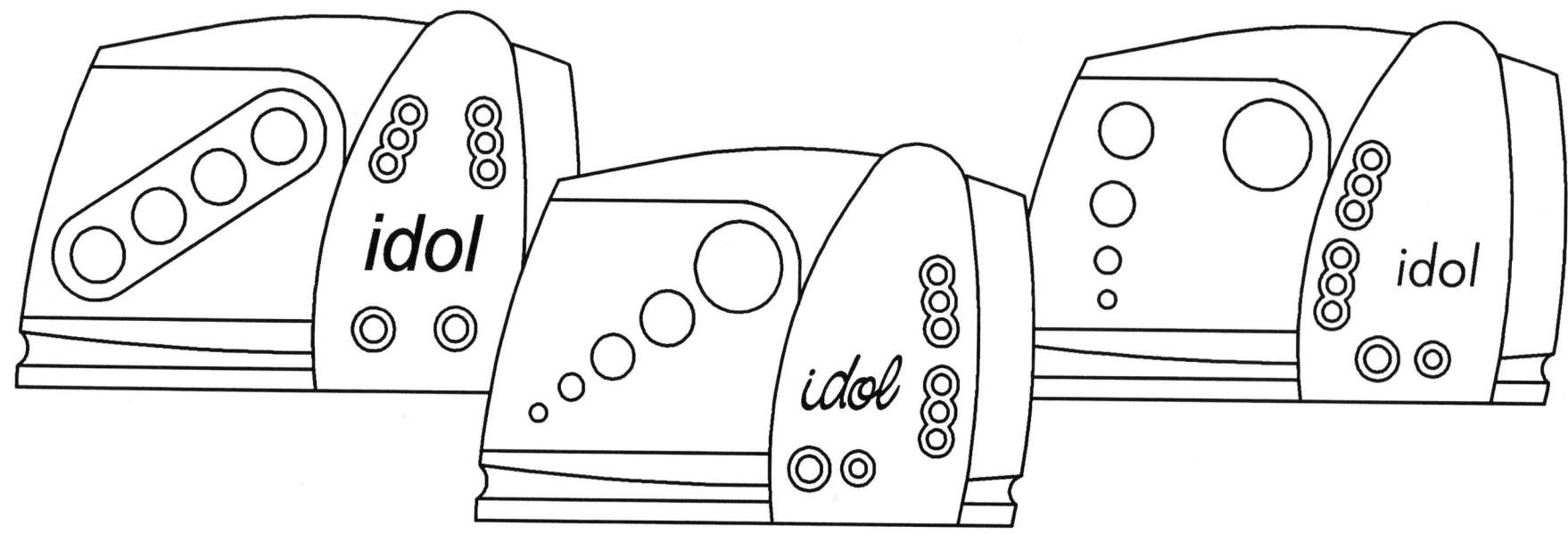

Layout variations of buttons, text, etc.

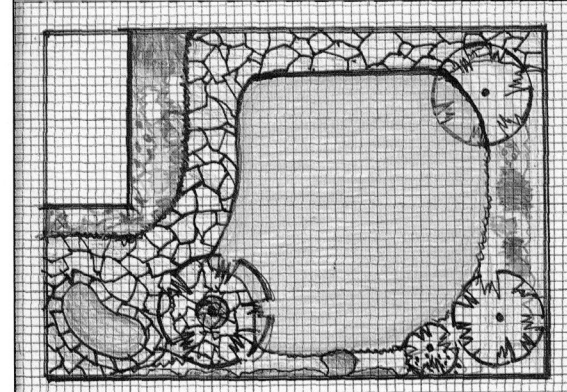

A useful way to work out the design of a large space, such as a room layout, stage set or garden, is to use a plan of the area.

Initial ideas can be easily drawn on graph paper using the squares to estimate the size and proportions of the space and features that you want to fit into it. For more detailed development work, you will need to produce a **scale drawing**.

Scale drawings show an accurate, measured plan of the area with elevations and sections of any vertical structures. Room layouts are usually drawn to a large scale (1:50, where one centimetre represents half a metre). This enables you to show details of furniture and fittings.

The floor plan usually shows a slice through the room at about 1.5 metres from the ground. This enables you to include the position of windows and furniture on the plan. You can use symbols to represent doorways, windows and furniture. It is helpful to draw these symbols at the correct scale on separate pieces of card or paper. This allows you to move them about and explore different

arrangements very easily and quickly on your plan. If you want to draw on and colour the plan, it is a good idea to make several photocopies of the original and experiment on these.

Wall elevations show flat views of the walls in the room including the siting of furniture and fittings that will be positioned on, or in front of, the walls.

Planning Spaces

The squares on grid paper can act as a useful guide. Using a pencil, mark the outline on the grid paper. Now lay tracing paper over the top and draw in the lines neatly with drawing instruments. Use different line thicknesses for outside edges etc., so that your line drawing is easier to understand. You can use the plan as a guide to project lines for elevations. These are usually shown above the plan with any sections being placed to the right. It is helpful to mark the sides from which the elevations are viewed on the plan itself.

You can show any ceiling features, such as the positioning of lights, by making a tracing paper overlay that mirrors the floor plan.

The scale is usually recorded in the bottom right-hand corner.

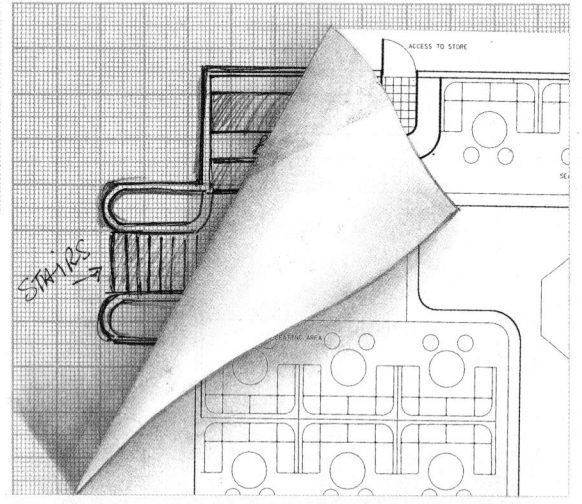

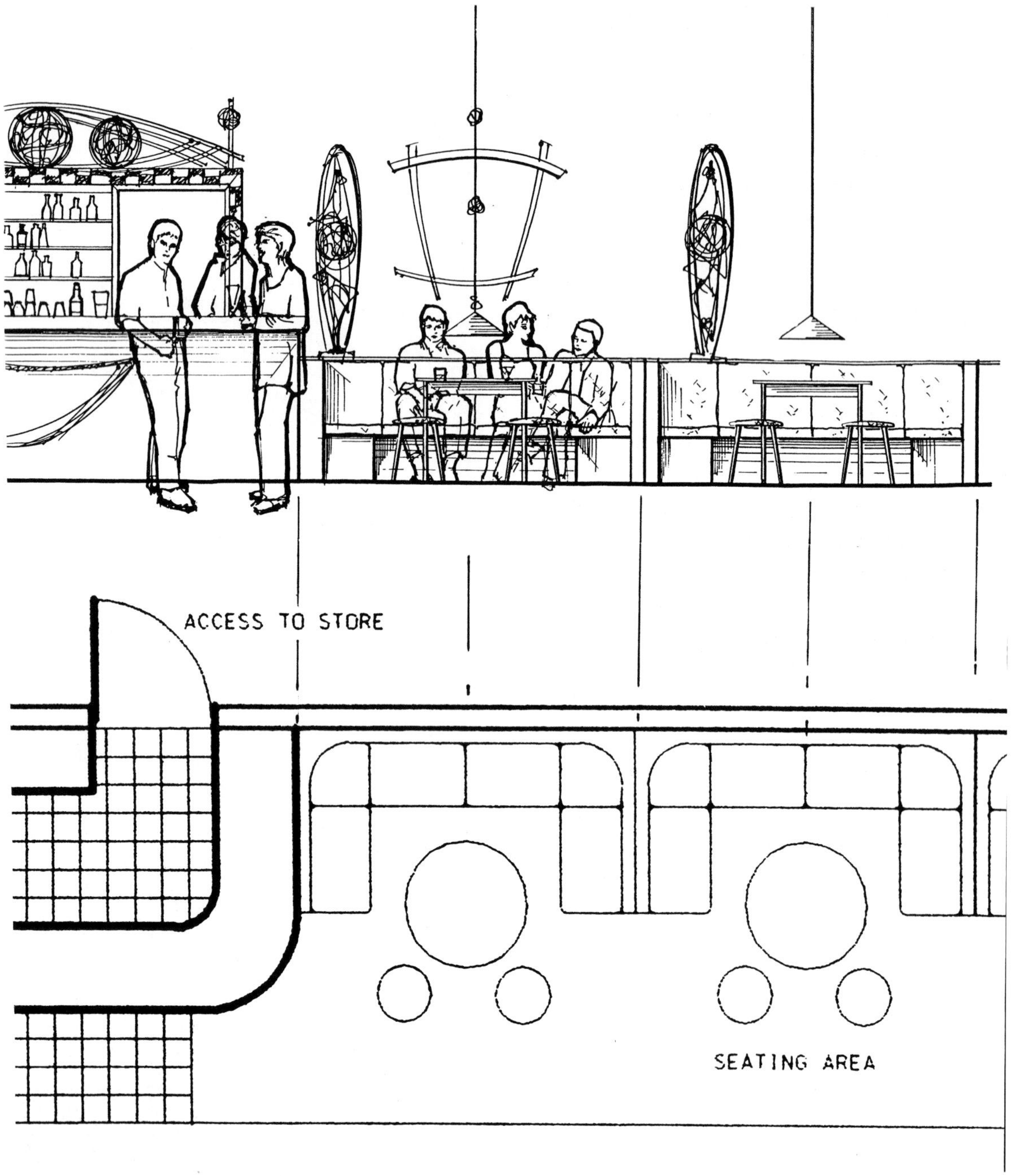

ACCESS TO STORE

SEATING AREA

Exploded drawings allow objects to be drawn where all the individual parts can be seen, giving an impression of how they fit together. This can prove very useful in explaining your ideas and giving a clearer indication of the parts that go together to create the finished product. It is also helpful in solving construction problems prior to manufacture.

Although they look quite complicated to produce, it can be a simple and quick process. Start by producing a sketch of the front and side elevations of the design, which should be exploded. This will guide you in producing an exploded view. Faintly draw in construction and centre lines to ensure that all components line up with each other. From this, it will then be possible to start constructing the perspective exploded view, constructing the boxes that contain individual components.

Try not to space out individual parts too much as the perspective will be distorted.

Exploded views can be drawn in one or two point perspective.

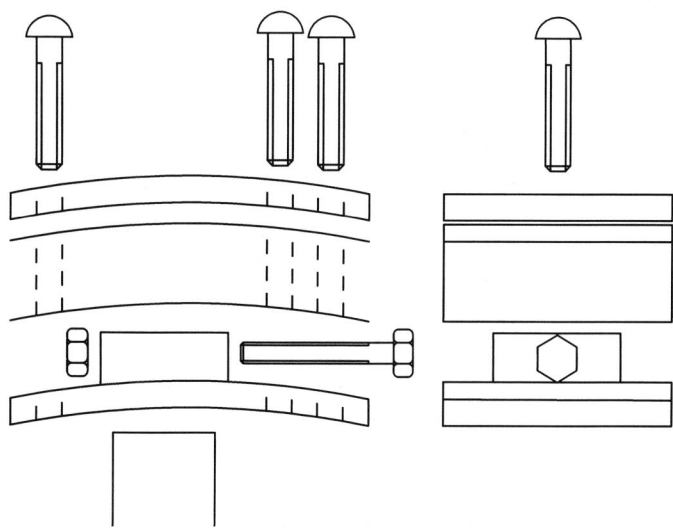

Exploded orthographic views

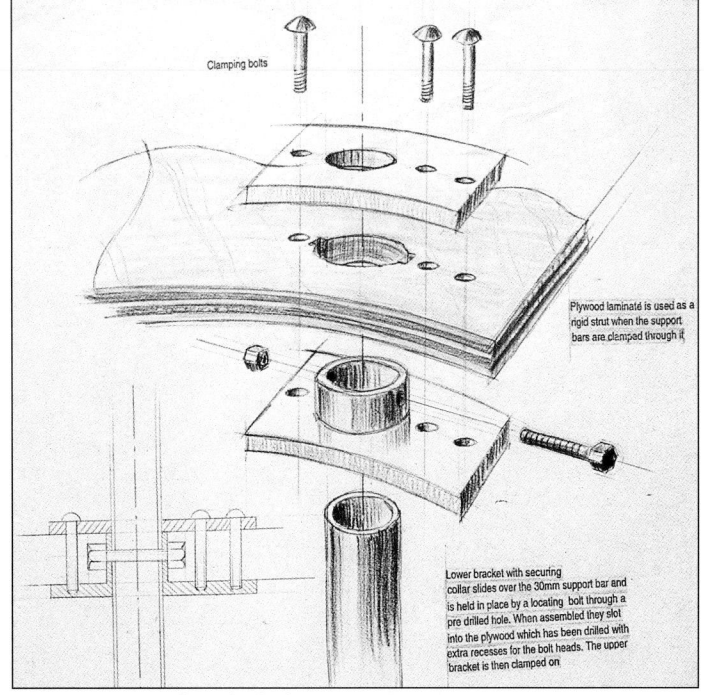

Construction of exploded perspective view

Sections

It may be necessary, at some stage of the modelling process, to show some form of hidden detail without having to explode the design. This can be done in a number of ways but most commonly through **sections** or **cutaways**. These allow the observer to view the inside of an object in order to gain a clearer picture of what is happening. This type of modelling is usually done in two dimensions but can also be constructed in three dimensions.

To construct a section, the point of interest is 'cut' as if it is being sliced open. This will expose a number of things that will help to give a clearer picture of how the object is constructed, such as material thickness and change in surface direction.

When working in two dimensions, it is standard practice to 'hatch' the surfaces that have been cut at 45 degrees to show that they represent a section. These can then be used in conjunction with other drawings, such as orthographic and perspective, to provide all the information you need about the object.

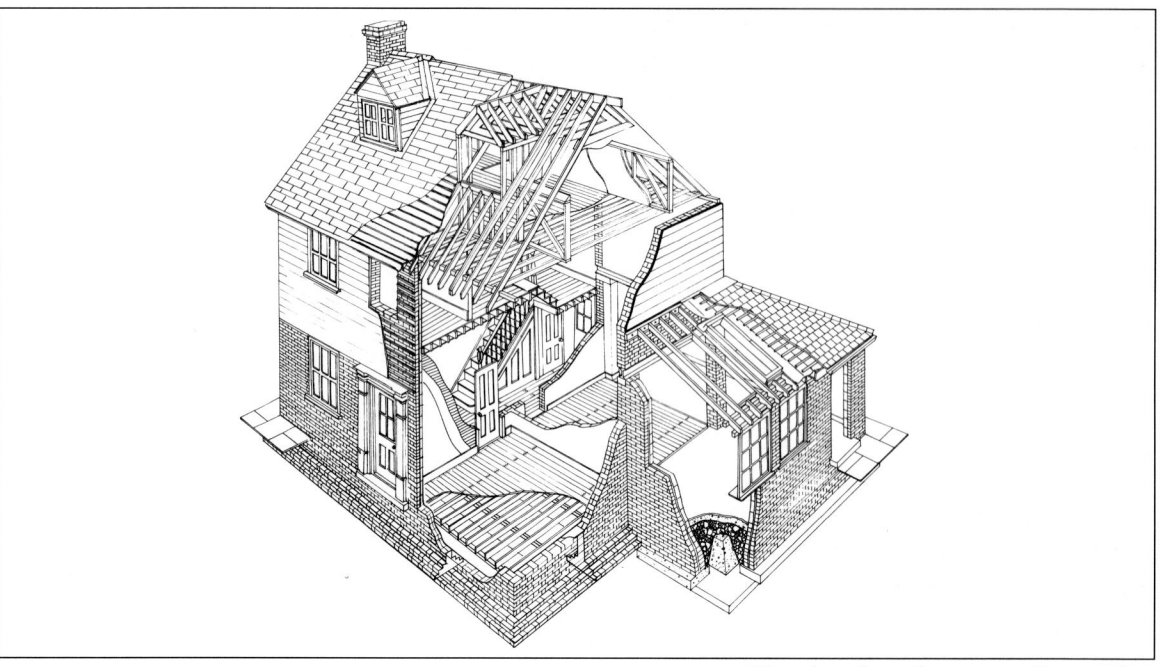

Line drawing of a perspective section

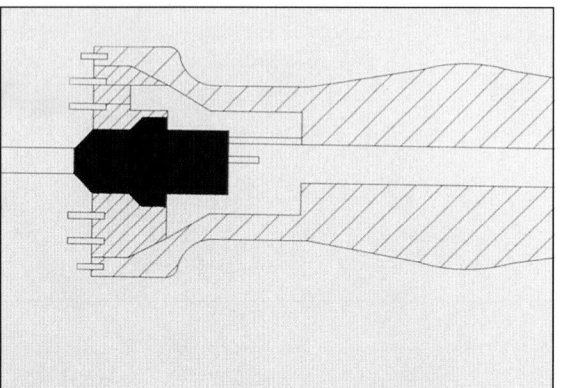

Hatched sections

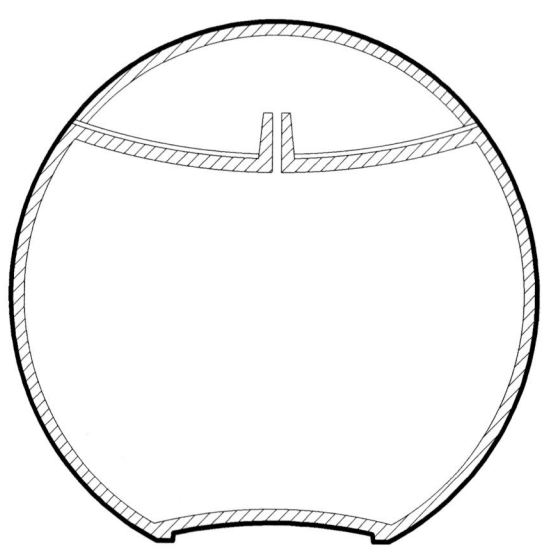

Aromatherapy oil dispenser in cross section

Cutaways are similar to sections but are usually viewed in three dimensions either in a perspective drawing or in a solid model.

This type of modelling can be quite difficult and models will require care in their construction. However, it can be a very descriptive way of showing how an object works, or is constructed.

If a cutaway is to be useful, it is important that the parts to be cut should expose an area of the interior that provides information about the product. This could show internal construction or expose mechanical or electronic parts to give a clearer picture of how the object functions.

When drawing two point perspective cutaways, it is important to construct the main exterior body of the product using measured perspective (see page 72–73). This method will prevent any error being seen as the interior is exposed.

Internal detailing can then be lightly drawn in, using the same method, projected from the elevations. When you have decided which area is to be cut away, draw this in. This will give you a clear picture of the exterior and the interior that is to be exposed.

As an alternative to cutaways, hidden details can be drawn in using dotted lines to show those parts that cannot be seen.

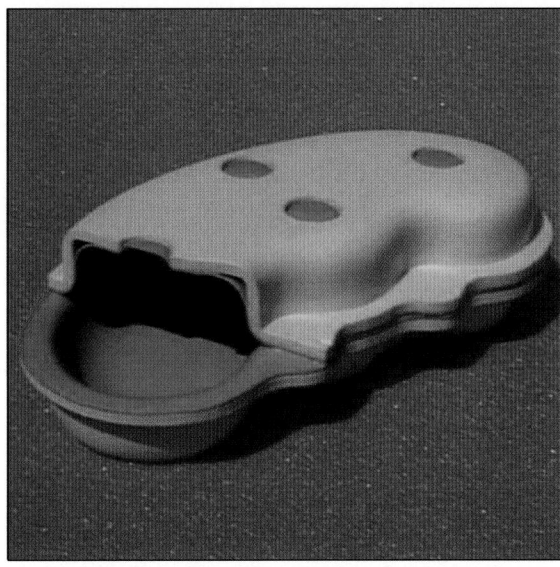

Cutaway through a model of a spectacle case

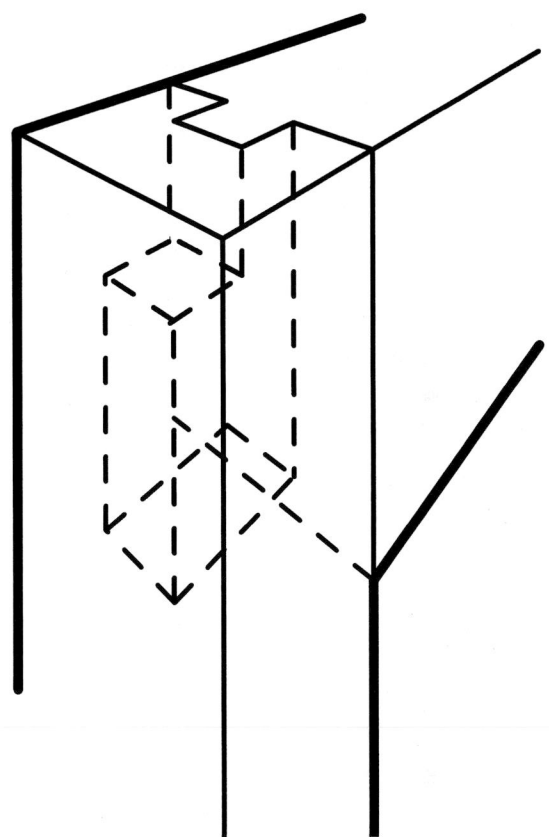

Hidden detail of a haunched mortice and tenon joint

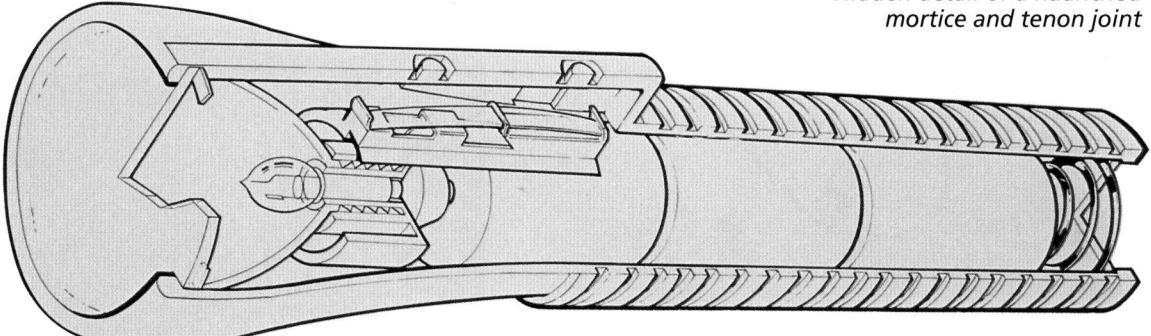

CAD / CAM

The use of computer aided manufacturing systems allows us to make components rapidly and accurately. This can be helpful as complicated shapes can be made and put together quickly to create 3D forms.

When a block model is being made, it is usually necessary to laminate sufficient material (MDF or a suitable timber) to make up a slightly larger block than the overall size of the model. This is then shaped and formed to achieve a final shape.

Computer aided design and manufacturing systems can make this process much quicker.

If we look at a working drawing of a product, we will be able to see the profile of the section in either front, side or plan views. We can take one of these views and generate the profile using CAD. If, as in this example, we draw the end elevation, the plan or front elevations will give us its length. In this case it is 150 mm.

With 15 mm thick MDF, the profile will have to be made 10 times. Once this is done, these can be glued together to form the block model. The only problem with this is that the 10 pieces will have to be aligned accurately. To make this process easier, include two holes in the CAD drawing so that they can be machined at the same time as the profiles are cut. If a steel rod or wooden dowel is passed through the holes when the pieces are being glued together, they will align accurately.

The block will now have the correct profile in two of its dimensions with the third being finished by hand and machine processes.

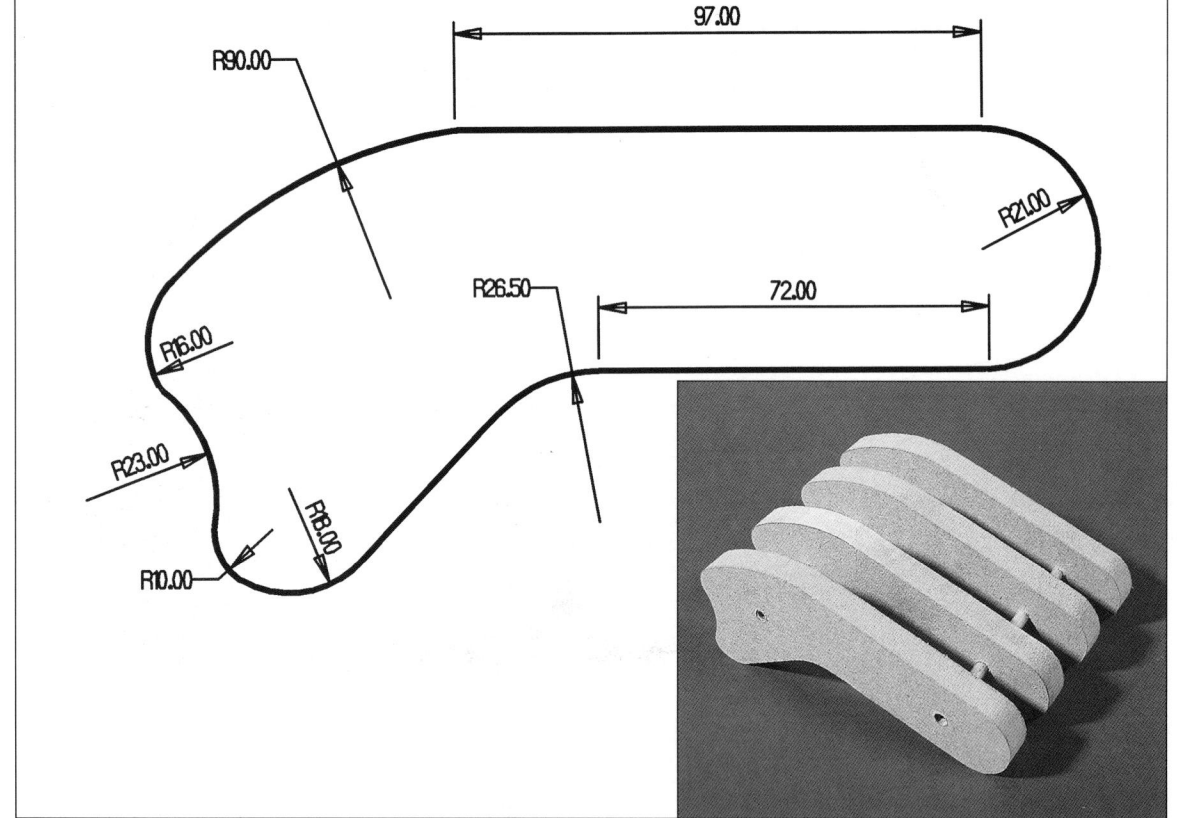

Basic orthographic drawing of a camera

Components aligned with rods

Finished model for a camera

To get closer to the finished three-dimensional shape it is possible to take sections at different points along the length of the object. This will give us a series of stepped profiles which, when glued together, will be nearer the finished shape but will still require some hand finishing. The thinner the material being used to cut individual profiles, the nearer to the finished shape the block will be.

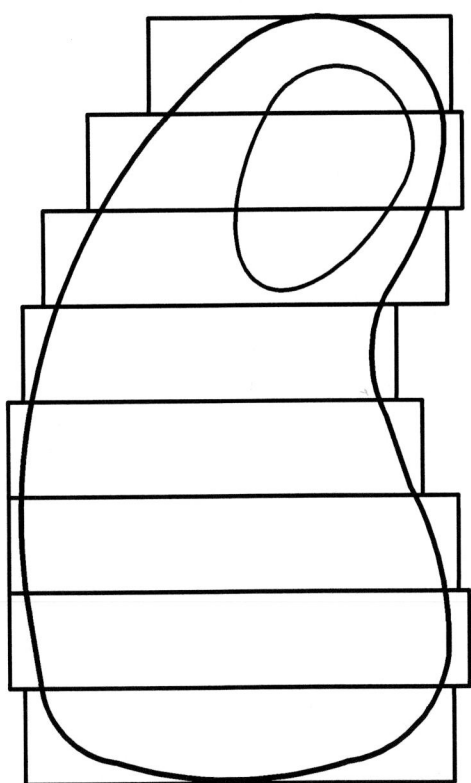

Basic orthographic drawing of personal stereo showing section outlines

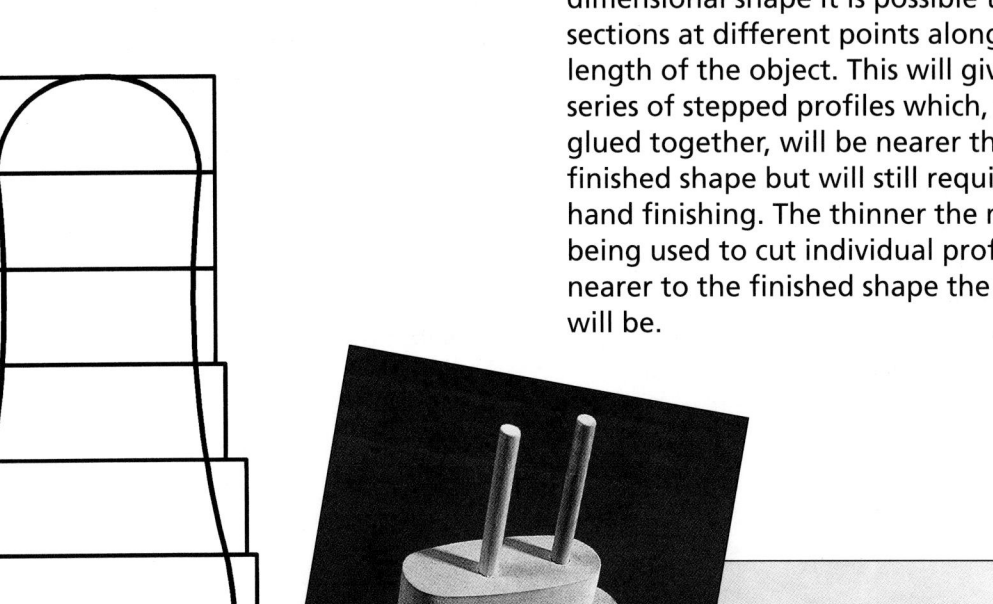

Components aligned with rods

Finished model of personal stereo

Wireframes

Three-dimensional wireframe models give a more realistic impression of an object than those created by extruding a two-dimensional image. They allow a clearer view of the product with all curves, facets and undercuts being displayed.

A big advantage of this type of modelling is that the view that is shown on screen can be changed as if the object is hanging in space and you are walking around it. This allows the designer to view the drawing from all angles so that its form, proportion and detailing can be assessed from every point prior to the addition of colour or texture.

The wireframe model can then be used to give a more realistic impression of the finished object, by giving it surface texture and making it look solid in form. If, for instance, the product is made from a plastic injection moulding, then this type of surface texture can be applied. The image can then be manipulated to give the most advantageous view to the observer.

Alternatively, the wireframe model can be used in conjunction with other drawings to produce a foam or wooden model in the workshops. The wireframe image can also be used, at a later stage, as a working underlay for rendering.

While this type of software is more appropriate for the advanced computer user, they usually have a standard set of pre-drawn three-dimensional objects which can be assembled and manipulated quite easily.

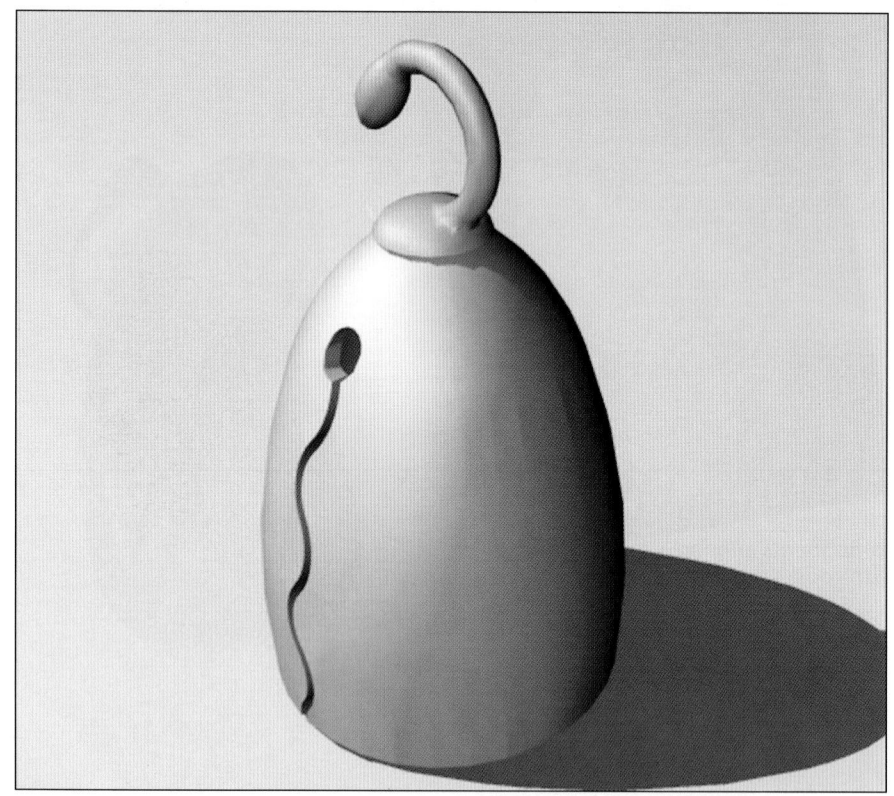

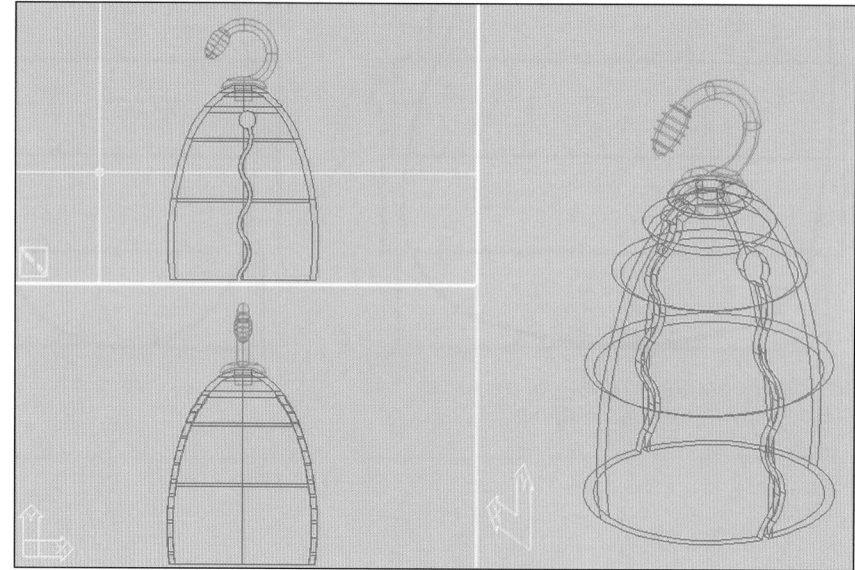

CAD image for a device to keep socks in pairs in the wash

Morphing in computer modelling is the process of gradually changing one image into another through animation. Both the starting image and the end image are needed for this process. You have probably seen very complex examples of morphing in the films *Terminator 2* and *The Mask.*

There are two different types of morphing software: two dimensional and three dimensional.

In two-dimensional morphing a 'warp' is specified that will show how the first image will be distorted into the second. Because this method uses flat images, hidden details will not be seen during the morphing process. When the animation is created, the stills from it will show variations of the two images.

Three-dimensional morphing is more complex in its process but works in a similar way in that the 3D models used as the start and end points will be morphed to create intermediate 3D models in the animation. These images can then be treated like any other computer generated 3D model.

Morphing can be useful in developing the visual form of products. If you have two different ideas for a product and use them in the morphing process, the stills that create the animation may show you some interesting variations on your initial ideas.

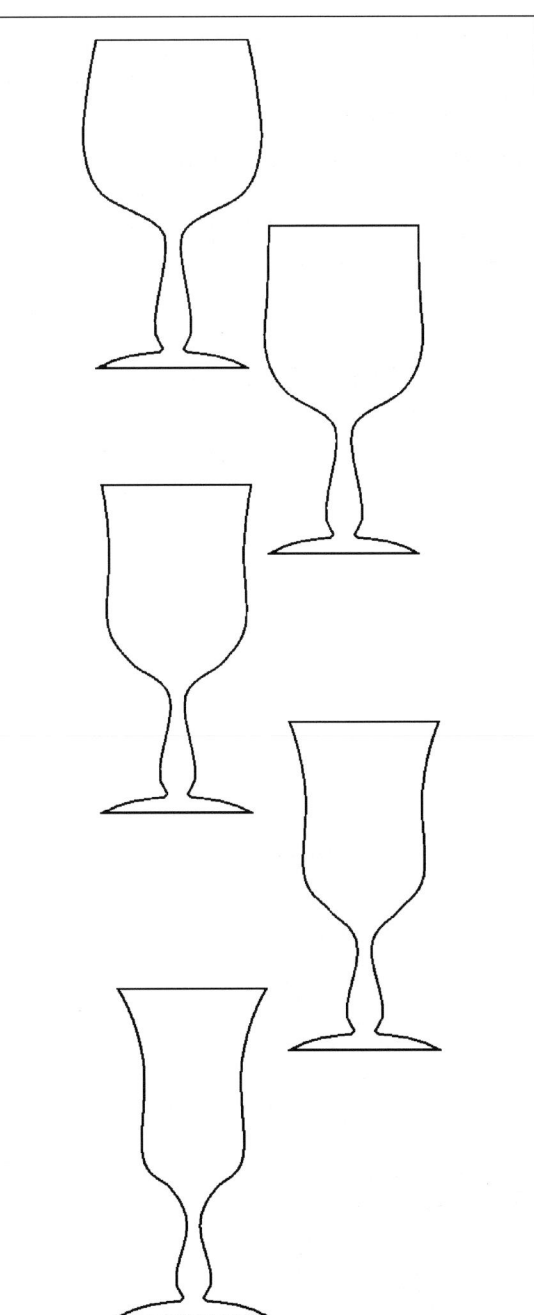

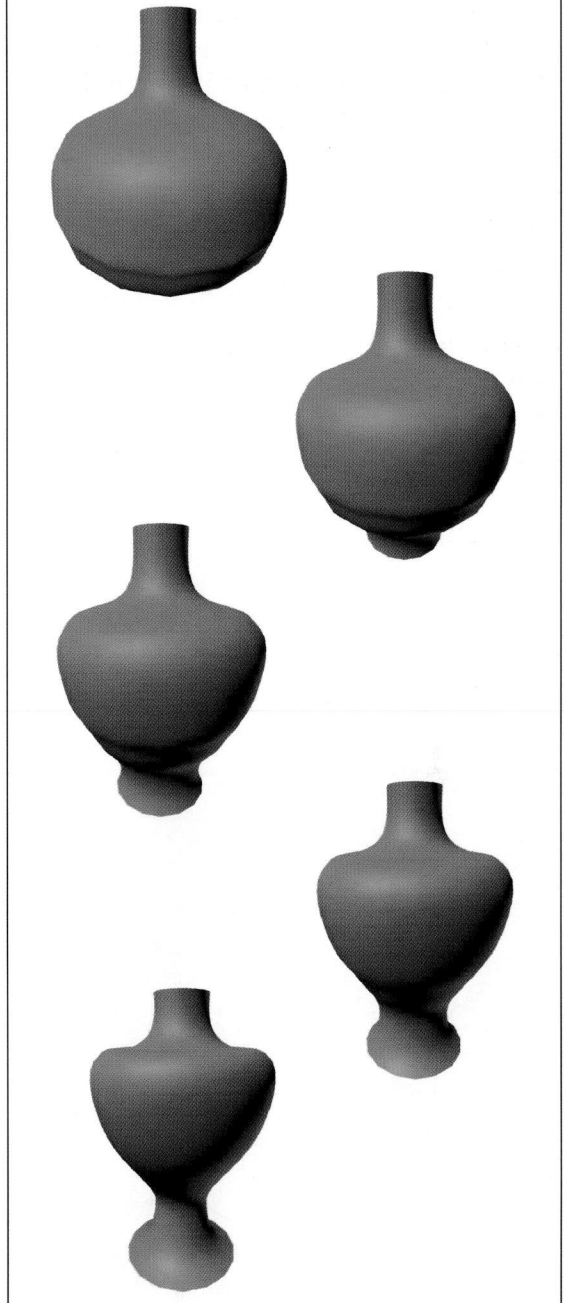

Presenting Ideas

The aim of a design presentation is to communicate the value of your ideas to the client in the most convincing way possible. To do this effectively, professionals use a variety of techniques:

- 2D and 3D presentation drawings
- Engineering drawings
- Detail drawings of parts of the design
- Small-scale and full-scale models
- Photographs
- Computer-based presentations
- Verbal presentations
- Written reports.

The choice of technique depends on three things, the **client's needs**, the **information** to be presented and the **nature of the product**.

THE CLIENT

Use a method of presentation that is suitable for the client, and the time and money available for the job. If they have asked for a limited restyling of an existing product, the presentation may be quite simple – perhaps consisting of presentation drawings showing the visual changes. However, if your client is a town council and the product is a new sports centre, your presentation will be more complex and could use most of the techniques listed above. Treat the planning of the presentation as a design exercise and write a specification listing all the information the client will need to know. Once this has been done, you can decide on the techniques that will be most effective in communicating your design.

THE INFORMATION

The presentation techniques used should suit the information you need to present. For example, manufacturing details could be explained by a series of engineering drawings, whereas information about costings would probably be presented more effectively in a written report. Be clear about exactly what you need to present and then choose techniques that will help the client to understand what you are trying to say.

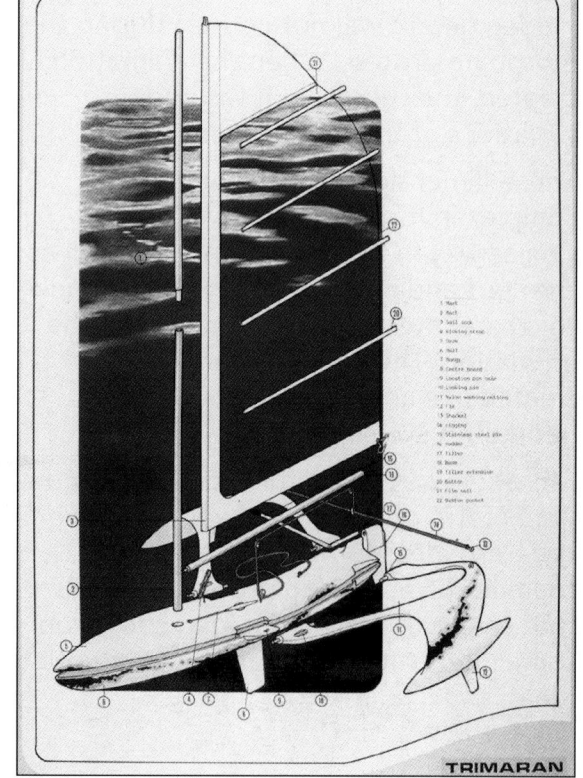

TRIMARAN

THE PRODUCT

You must also consider the character of the product. As a designer it is essential that your presentation is convincing and visually stimulating. It is often a good idea to use a style of presentation to support the image of the product. In this way, a playground climbing frame might be presented in the kind of simple, colourful style that is sometimes used for children's book illustrations, whereas a piece of high-tech sports equipment might benefit from a more technical treatment.

The following pages show a variety of techniques that you can use to create exciting presentations. Play to your strengths and gradually introduce new skills to your presentations as you become confident in their use. Remember that a well thought out presentation will help the client to understand and appreciate your ideas, whereas careless work can have the opposite effect.

A cartoon-style visual has been used to introduce the idea of a portable ice-cream vending machine

Scale model used to present the design of an office reception area

Coloured Pencils

Coloured pencils tend to be undervalued. They are probably the least expensive, yet one of the most useful, items you will find in your graphics kit. They give instant, long-lasting colour and are quick to use, easy to control and involve no mess.

They can be bought individually or in boxed sets. Choose pencils that are soft enough to produce even shading yet will not snap when you need to create a crisp line. Some of the poorer quality crayons are hard and gritty and have weak colour intensity. These really are a waste of money and will spoil your drawings.

Try mixing crayons to create a wider range of colours or experiment with pencil pressure to vary the tone (light and dark).

Pencil crayon may be rubbed on to the page to give a smooth area of subtle colour. They are excellent for adding detail and highlights to marker or pastel drawings.

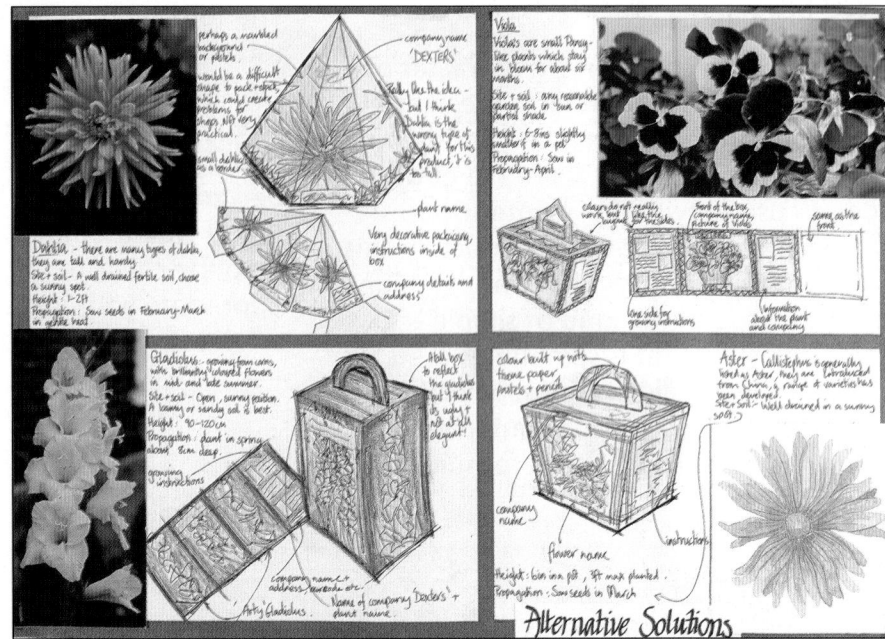

1

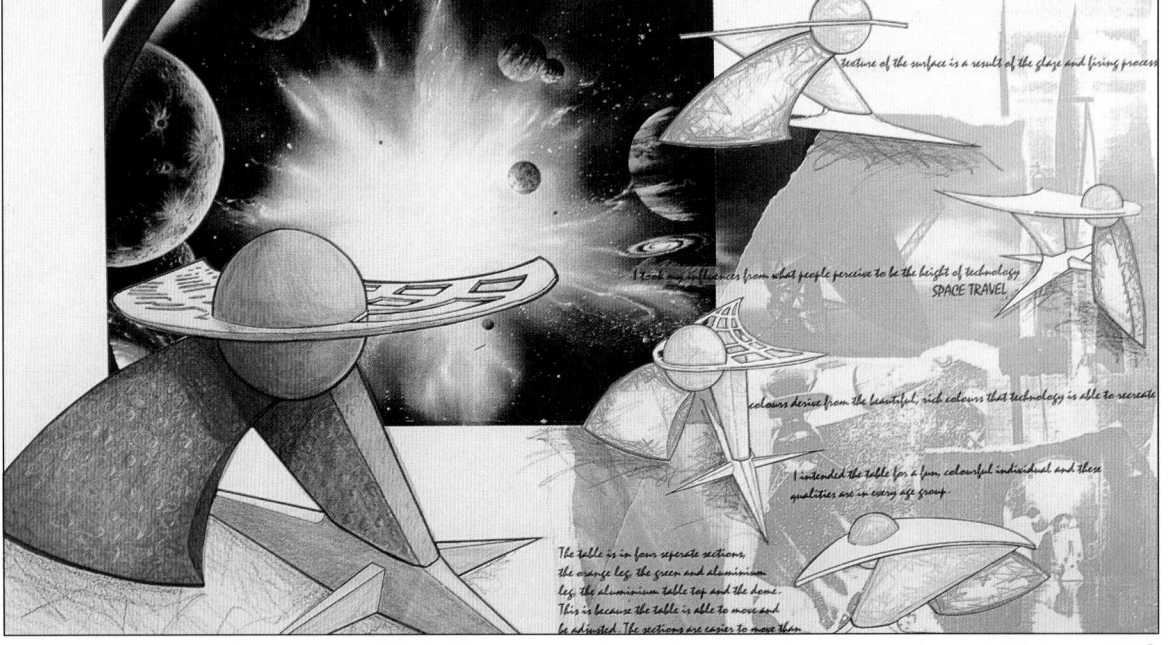

Fig. 1
Research and early ideas for bulb and seed packaging

Fig. 2
Pencil crayon used on top of marker to create texture

2

WATER-SOLUBLE CRAYONS

These are really worth experimenting with. They are a type of pencil crayon that can be mixed with water to produce a similar effect to water colour paints. In dry form they behave as normal, soft pencil crayons but will dissolve when mixed with water. They can be used to produce flat 'washes' of colour or blended and mixed on the page with a brush to give strong colours and an interesting paint-like quality. They are particularly suitable for drawing natural objects or fabric-soft materials that require a more organic look.

NOTE: If the paper becomes too wet it will tend to wrinkle, so it is advisable to use a heavy water colour paper or you may need to stretch the paper (see Water-based Paints, page 85).

A tile design in water-soluble crayons

Measured Perspective

Measured perspective is a technical way of drawing your design and gives a more accurate perspective view. Although there are a number of ways to do this type of two point perspective drawing, this method (called measured point) is fairly straight forward. The image is created with the aid of a front and side elevation.

The first stage is to establish the eye line with its two vanishing points. Next, locate the observation point which will determine which side of the object you see the most of. If it is closer to the right-hand vanishing point, you will see more of the left-hand side of the object, and vice versa. The angle of the two lines at this point should be 90°.

At this point you can either draw in or overlay the front and side elevations as shown (Fig. 1).

Next, establish a ground line. Its position will determine how much of the top of the object you see. The closer the line is to the observation point, the more of it will be visible (Fig. 2).

With these points and lines established, you should now draw in a height line which is vertical and runs through the observation point. The point where this line meets the ground line will be the front bottom corner of your image and so the first two perspective (base) lines can be put in by drawing back to the vanishing points.

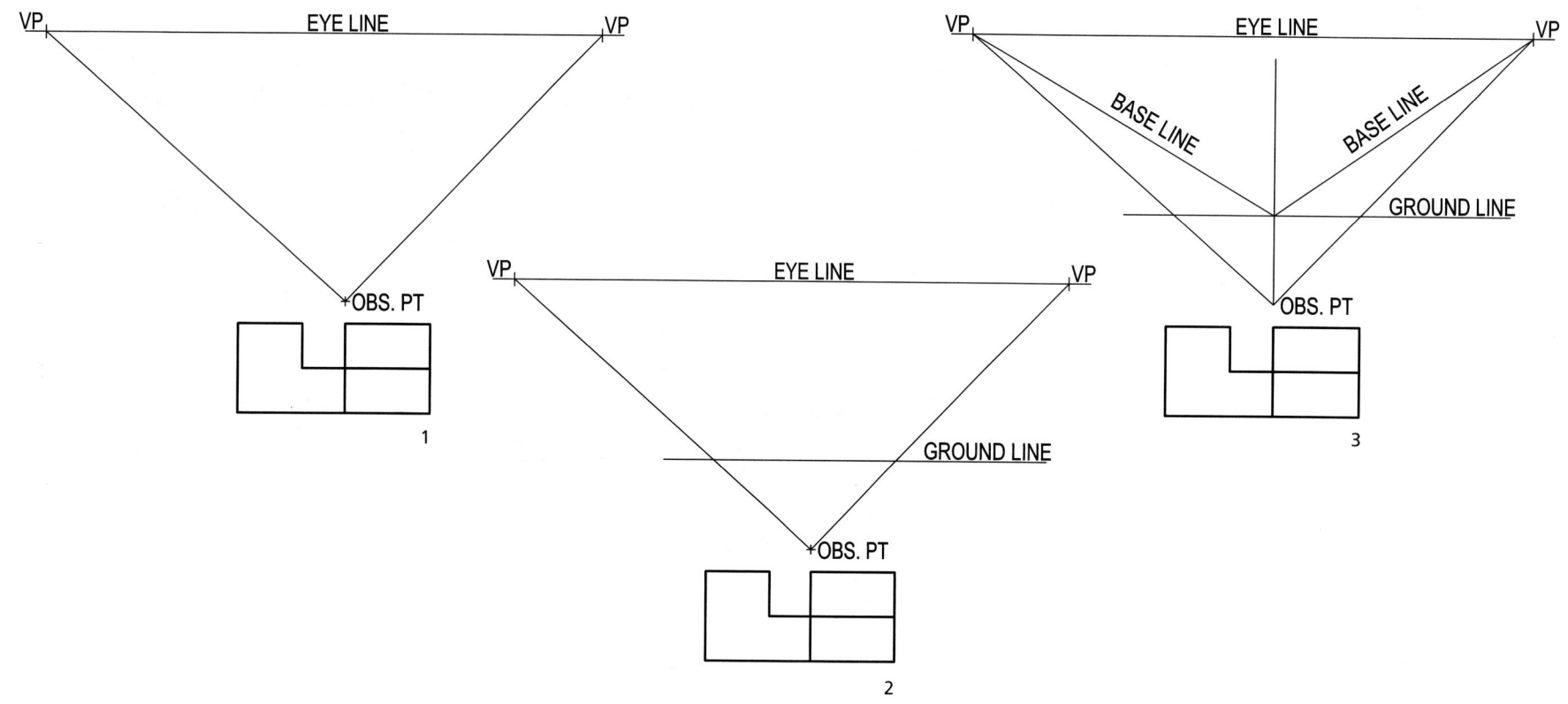

To find the measuring points, use a compass to draw two arcs with the vanishing points as their centres. The arcs should pass through the observation point (Fig. 1). The points where the arcs meet the eye line will give you the measuring points. Mark them LMP (left measuring point) and RMP (right measuring point).

First establish the outline of the image.

The front vertical edge of the object can be drawn in at the scale being used. Its end point can then be projected back to the left- and right-hand vanishing points.

From the front elevation, project the left-hand edge vertically until it meets the ground line. From this point, project it back to the RMP. Where it crosses the base line will fix the length of this edge. The end point can be drawn vertically to complete this side of the object (Fig. 2).

Go through the same process to draw the right-hand side of the object. With this in position, you now have enough information to draw in the top.

All further lines are drawn in the same way.

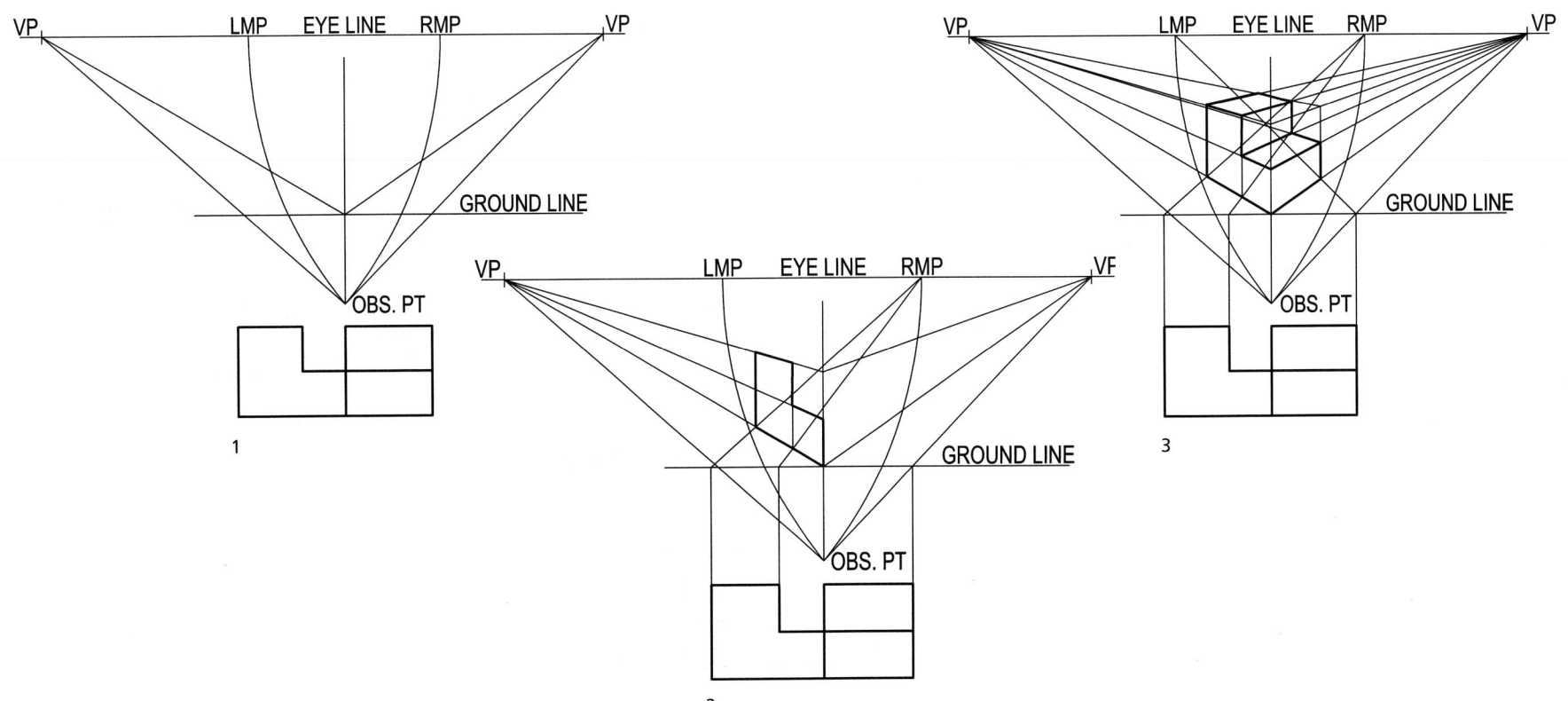

Coloured Paper

You can create an effective presentation drawing using simple shading on coloured papers such as Ingres or sugar paper.

- Select a background colour that will provide the mid tone for your drawing.

- Lightly draw in the outline using pencil crayon.

- Decide which direction the light is coming from. Use a pencil crayon or marker that is a darker tone than the background paper to mark in all the edges that are in shade.

- Draw in all of the edges facing the light with a white pencil crayon.

- Make your drawing come 'alive' by adding highlights with white gouache paint.

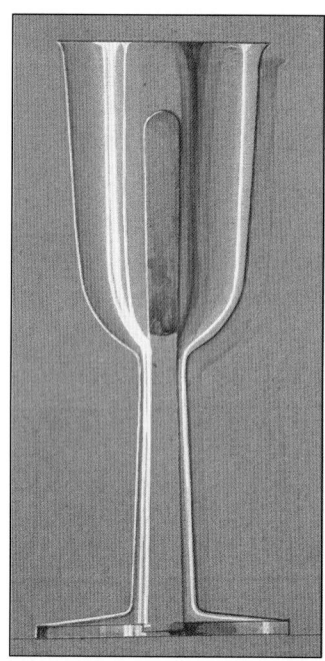
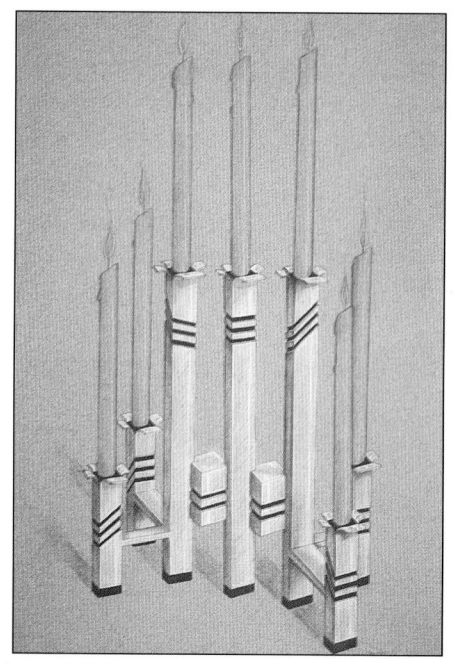

Coloured soft pastels give subtle colour to design drawings. In design rendering they are most often used in powder form, scraped from the stick, and applied to the page with cotton wool. This is a useful method for representing smooth surfaces such as plastics and metal. They can be used to draw directly onto the page but the crumbly colour is intense and difficult to control.

Pastels are made from powdered pigment bound together with a gum to produce a fragile stick of pure colour. They can be bought as boxed sets or individually.

Be wary of poor quality cheap sets as these may be hard and gritty and will not perform well in powdered form.

Pastels are very adaptable and can be blended to mix extra colours or smudged to create different effects. Colour can be lifted using an eraser to neaten up edges or to produce bright highlights.

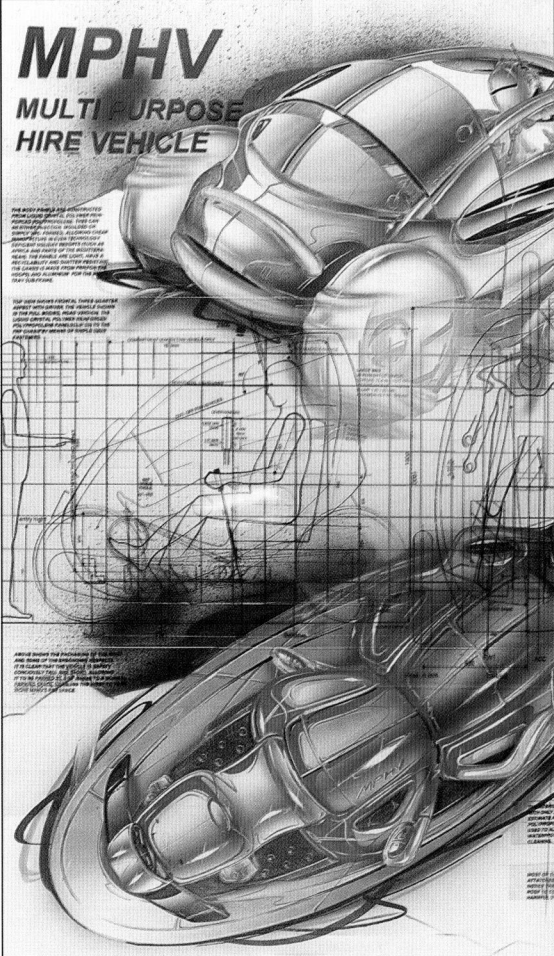

Presentation drawings using soft pastels, markers and gouache

Soft Pastels and Oil Pastels

These are generally used with other media such as markers or pencil crayons or diluted with solvents to create exciting background effects.

As you become experienced at using pastels you will find that you can produce an impressive presentation drawing with a polished 'air-brushed' quality.

FIXATIVES

As pastels are so delicate, it is important to protect your drawing with a fixative spray to help prevent the drawing from smudging. A light coat of fixative spray or 'hair spray' will help to fix the pastel dust to the page. Do not overdo the spraying as the fixative can tend to dull the drawing.

OIL PASTELS

These are a very different type of colouring stick. They are closer to wax crayons, having an oily waxy texture. They are not suitable for scraping and will not produce a dust or powder film. Oil pastels will give vibrant colour and interesting textures. They are most effective on coloured paper and can be used for interesting backgrounds.

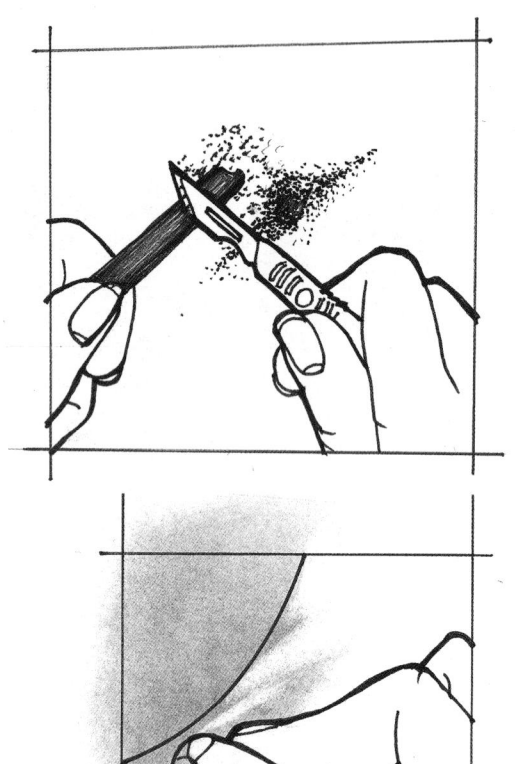

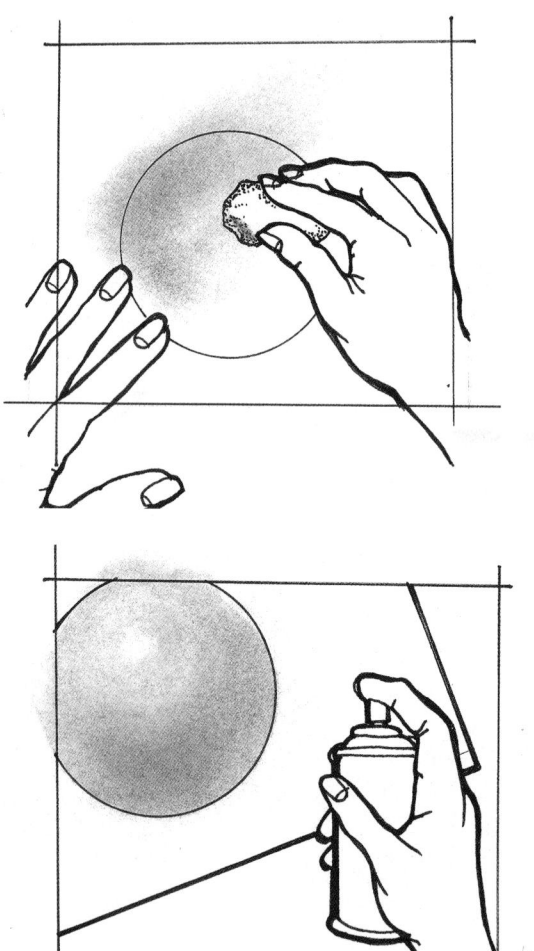

Fashion drawing in oil pastel

Marker pens are popular with designers as they offer a wide range of colours that are fast drying and convenient to use. In many ways they have replaced paint as a method of colouring drawings. New types of markers are continually being developed with different types of inks and varying shapes of tip. The main categories of marker are: **fine line markers**, **felt-** or **fibre-tips** and **studio markers**.

Fine line markers are available in different tip sizes to give a variety of line thickness. They are easier to use than technical pens but can still produce a degree of accuracy. They are also ideal for quick sketching or for writing notes and annotating design drawings.

Felt- or fibre-tip pens are usually sold as large brightly-coloured sets and have an image of being 'cheap and cheerful'. Unfortunately, the loud garish colours of these pens have a limited use in design drawings and the water-based inks are difficult to apply evenly.

Fine line markers used in product and jewellery design development work.

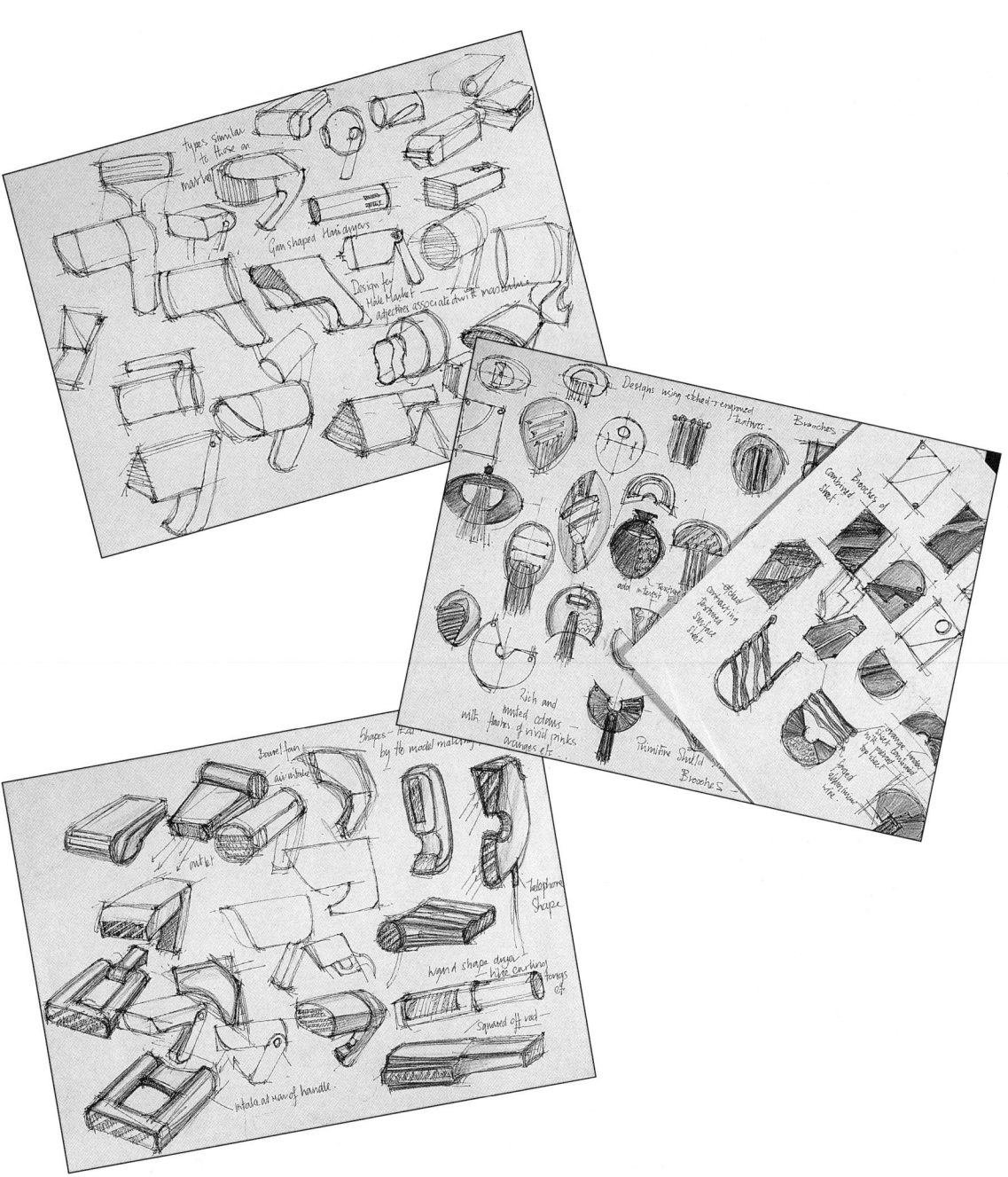

Marker Pens

Studio markers are available in a huge variety of colours and shades. They have specially designed tips for different types of work and are of a better quality than the less expensive felt tips. The two main types contain either spirit- or solvent-based ink or water-based ink.

Spirit- or solvent-based markers are quick drying and give a smooth flow of ink to produce flat areas of colour. They do tend to 'bleed' or soak through the paper so it is advisable to work on top of scrap paper or to use marker paper that has a special coating designed to avoid some of the problems of 'bleeding'.

Water-based markers can be obtained in a wide selection of colours. They do not tend to give the quality of finish of spirit-based markers and can wrinkle the surface of thin paper if overworked.

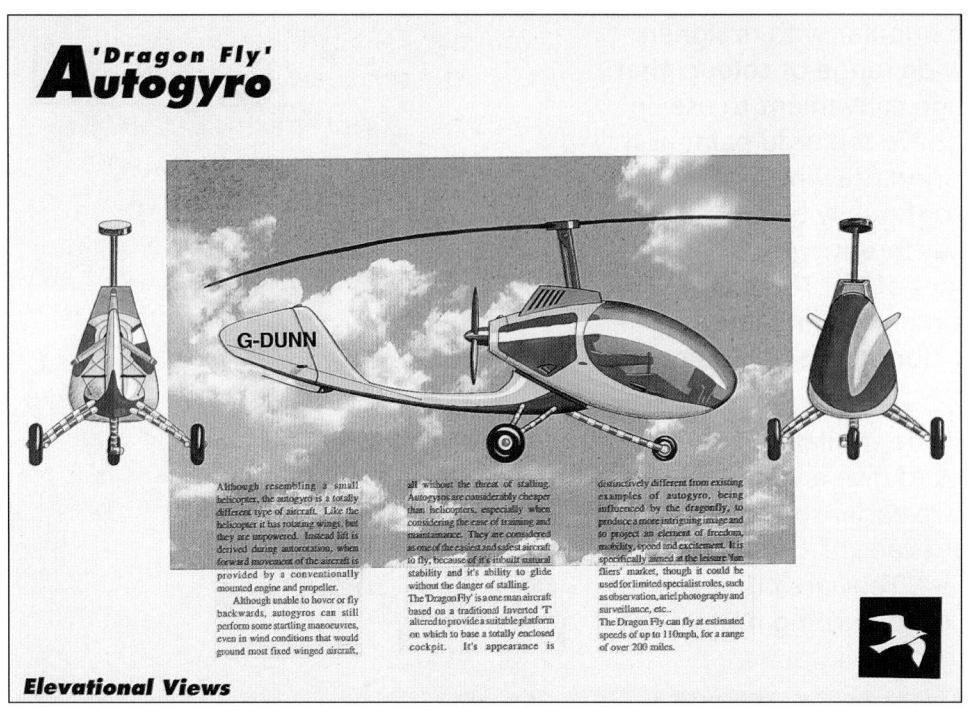

A 'Dragon Fly' **utogyro**

G-DUNN

Although resembling a small helicopter, the autogyro is a totally different type of aircraft. Like the helicopter it has rotating wings, but they are unpowered. Instead lift is derived during autorotation, when forward movement of the aircraft is provided by a conventionally mounted engine and propeller.

Although unable to hover or fly backwards, autogyros can still perform some startling manoeuvres, even in wind conditions that would ground most fixed winged aircraft,

all without the threat of stalling. Autogyros are considerably cheaper than helicopters, especially when considering the ease of training and maintenance. They are considered as one of the easiest and safest aircraft to fly, because of it's inbuilt natural stability and it's ability to glide without the danger of stalling.

The 'Dragon Fly' is a one man aircraft based on a traditional Inverted 'T' altered to provide a suitable platform on which to base a totally enclosed cockpit. It's appearance is

distinctively different from existing examples of autogyro, being influenced by the dragonfly, to produce a more intriguing image and so project an element of freedom, mobility, speed and excitement. It is specifically aimed at the leisure 'fun fliers' market, though it could be used for limited specialist roles, such as observation, ariel photography and surveillance, etc..

The Dragon Fly can fly at estimated speeds of up to 110mph, for a range of over 200 miles.

Elevational Views

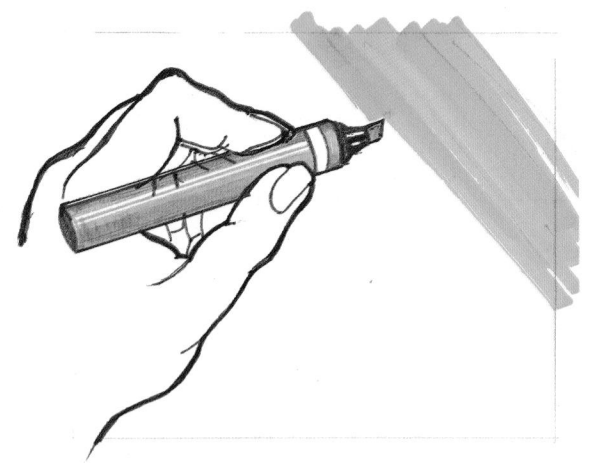

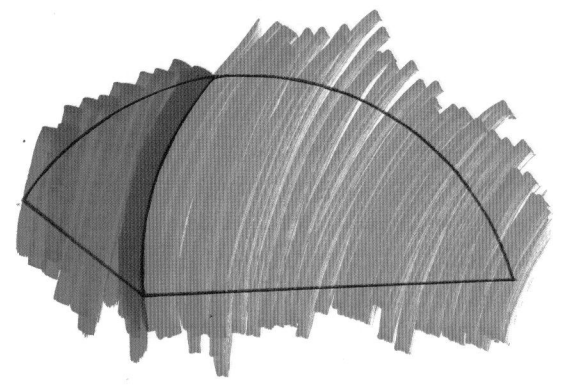

Colouring with markers takes practice as you must work quickly and boldly.

- Draw the outline in pencil. Work across the drawing stopping and starting outside pencil lines.

- Work quickly, keeping a wet edge so that the lines blend together. Do not rest the pen on the drawing as it will leave a darker blotch.

- To darken the tone let the first coat dry and then apply a second or third coat. You can add highlights with a white crayon or gouache when the ink is dry.

- Cut out with a scalpel and assemble parts using spray adhesive.

If you are buying markers for the first time it is not necessary to splash out and buy a large set. Select a few colours that you will find most useful. The light tones of neutral colours such as greys, blues and beiges are adaptable and easier to work with than the bold strong colours. A chisel-shaped tip is the most versatile and will produce a range of different line thicknesses.

Three Point Perspective

Although **three point perspective** is not used very often, it can create greater interest in 2D visuals. In some cases, adding a third perspective point makes the drawing look more realistic. We can make images appear to tower above us as if standing at the base of a building or make them appear to fall away to the ground when standing on top of them.

To see the effect that three point perspective can have on a drawing, start by producing a cube in two point perspective. You can experiment by moving the outside vertical lines in as if they were converging to a third point.

To construct a three point perspective image from scratch, the process is similar to that used in creating a two point perspective drawing.

This time though, add a third point at the bottom of your drawing, positioned centrally to the two points on the eye line.

With the ground line established, draw in the front edge of your object and then take the ends of this line back to the two vanishing points on the eye line. The difference this time is that rather than the vertical lines of the object remaining parallel, they will converge to the third vanishing point.

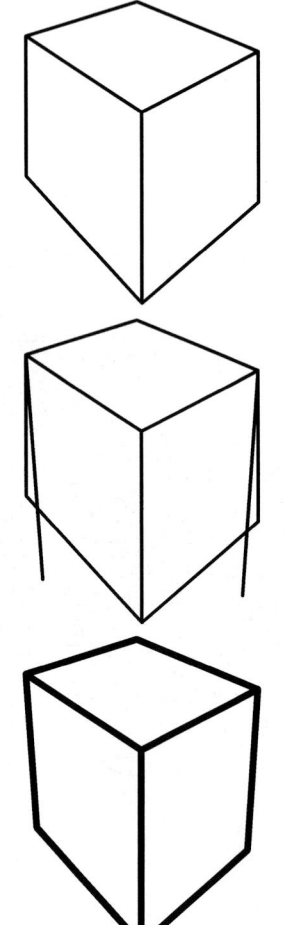

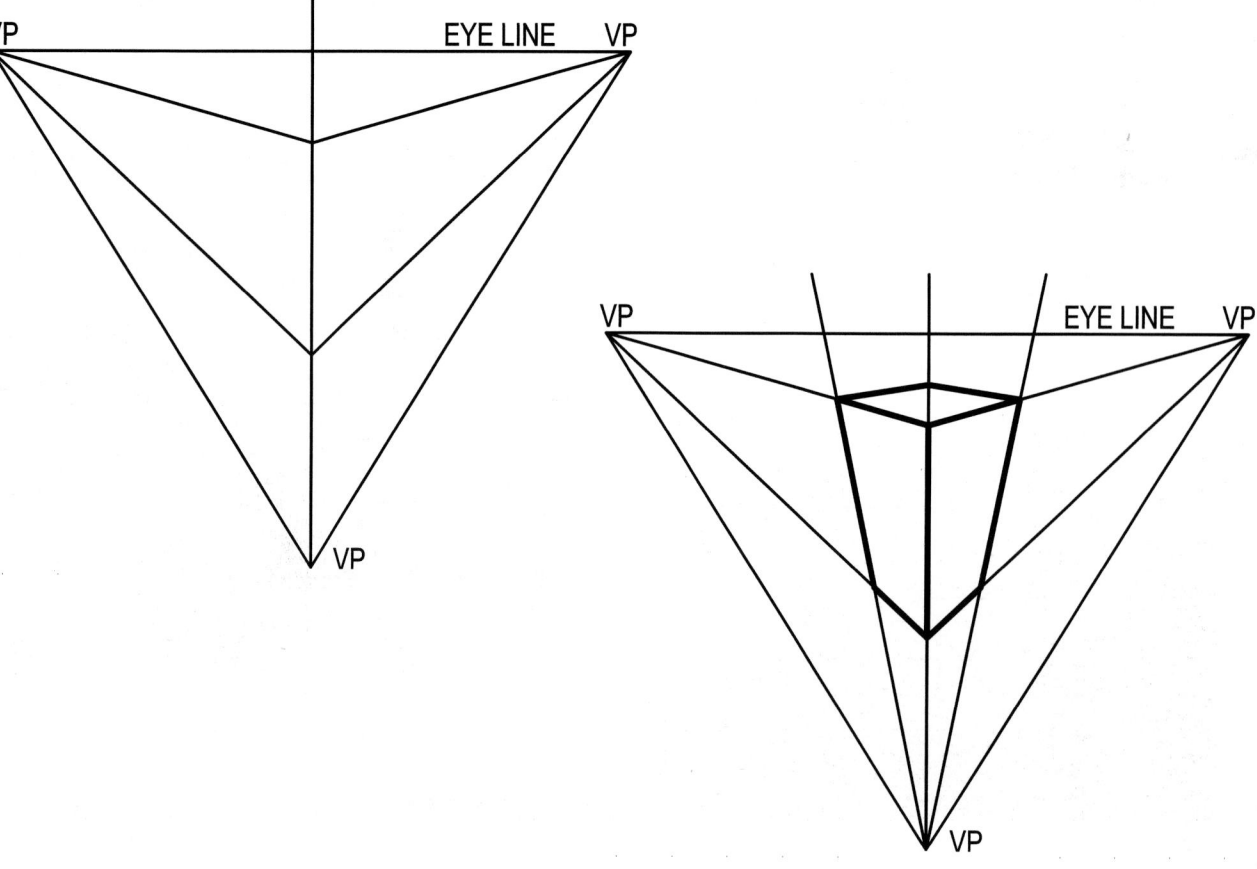

To produce an exploded presentation drawing, the process is the same as shown earlier (page 61) but there is clearly a need to produce a more accurate image. As well as using the orthographic drawing to aid construction, it is also helpful to have a perspective view of the finished product which can be used as an underlay.

With the underlay in position, you can begin to construct the exploded view. Initially, draw the construction lines in the direction of explosion (it may be helpful to 'crate' specific parts of the underlay to do this).

From this point, decide which area of your object is to remain static and lightly draw in this component.

Next, move the underlay so that the first exploded part is in position, using the construction lines as a guide. There will clearly be a difference between the size of the underlay and the construction lines because of the perspective, and so it will be necessary to adjust the exploded part to meet these lines. This part can then be lightly drawn in.

Proceed in this way, moving the underlay around for drawing individual exploded parts.

Care must be taken in deciding how far to explode individual components. As the parts get further away from the static component, the perspective view will tend to become distorted and so the view will have to be adjusted to accommodate this. In addition, if the parts are exploded so far that there is no overlapping, more of the hidden detail will have to be drawn, increasing the length of time necessary to complete the drawing.

'Dragon Fly'
Autogyro

1. Canopy
2. Cockpit insert- Pressure formed ABS
3. Starboard fuselage shell- Fibreglass
4. Airframe- Aluminium
5. Rotor mast
6. Rotor head
7. Head pitch control column
8. Engine position
9. Rear fuselage moulding
10. Rudder ground strike protector
11. Rudder monocoque
12. Engine access door
13. Rear undercarriage pylon
14. Rear wheel
15. Rear tyre
16. Port fuselage shell
17. Fuel tank- 9.5 gallon
18. Forward tyre
19. Forward wheel
20. Forward undercarriage pylon
21. Flight instrument consol

Exploded View

Cutaway Sections

In presenting a product there will usually be some part of it which will be hidden. Different types of cutaway model can be used to evaluate internal construction or visual and ergonomic features, while mechanical and electrical parts can be demonstrated through test models.

This example of a glue gun shows many of these features coming together in a two-dimensional cutaway presentation model. The designer has first shown a presentation drawing of the finished product and then shown it with one half of the outer casing removed to expose the interior. It shows how the internal components function in terms of the product's use. It also gives a clear understanding of structure and mountings.

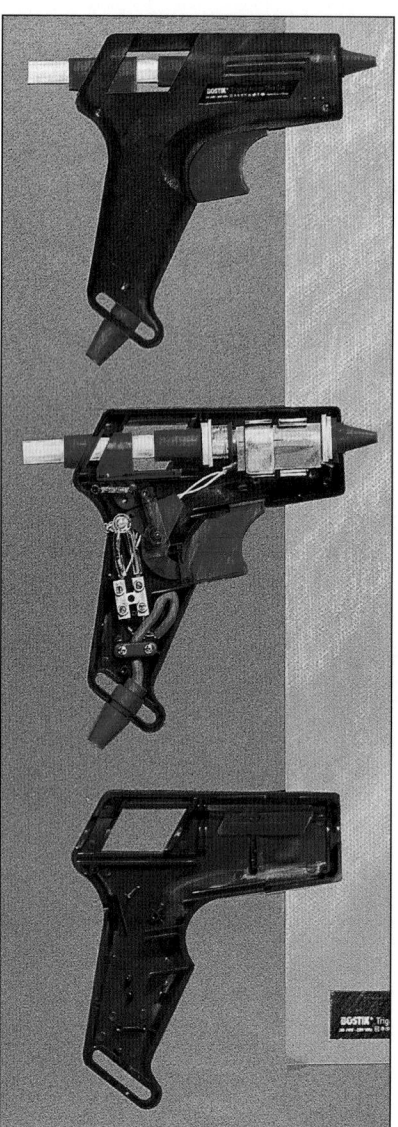

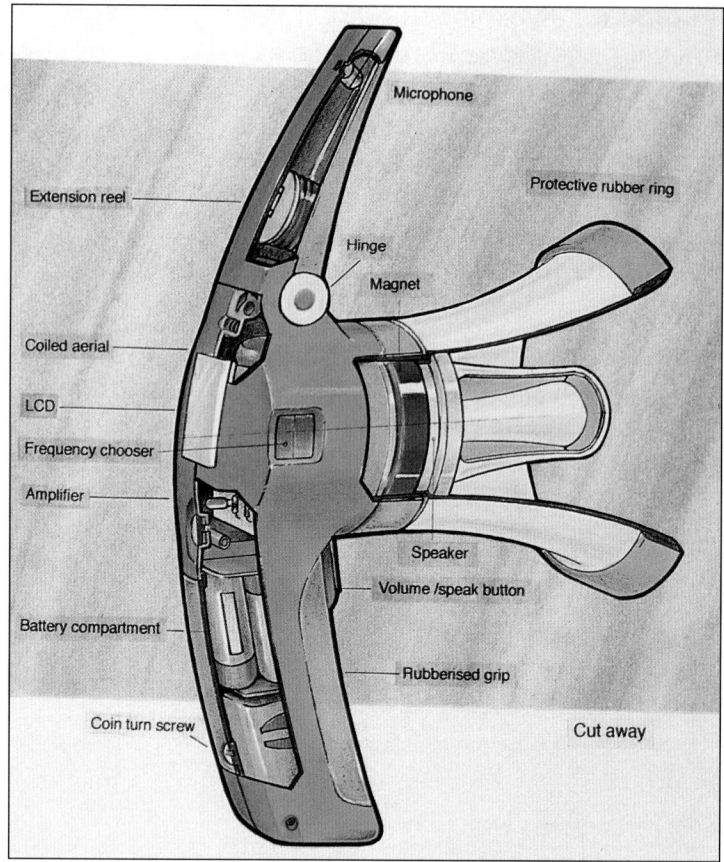

A further example, an event starter, was presented as a 3D block model with supportive 2D images. In this case, it was important that internal features could be shown to understand how the product would function. The designer chose to do this through a 2D model with various parts being 'cutaway'.

Airbrushes

The impressive illustrations on this page have been produced using an airbrush. The fine spray of colour can create soft graduations of tone to give a smooth photographic effect. Unfortunately, such complex drawings are time consuming to produce as the technique involves the use of stencils, and each stage of the colouring process needs to be planned.

Airbrushes can, however, be ideal for adding reflections and shine to drawings and for small-scale models.

All airbrushes work by mixing air (or gas) with droplets of paint to make a fine pressurised spray.

The cheapest method of obtaining compressed air is to use a car inner tube which has been fitted with an adapter for the air hose. You can also purchase small canisters of compressed air from art shops or use an air compressor.

The colours for the airbrush must be quite fine and fast drying so that they do not clog up the airbrush. Gouache, water colour, inks and acrylic are all suitable if thinned down to the consistency of milk. Whatever medium you use, it is essential to clean the airbrush thoroughly after use. If paint is left inside to dry, you will require special solvents to remove it.

1

2

Fig. 1 Airbrush illustration of a car

Fig. 2 Model sprayed with an airbrush

Fig. 3 Airbrush illustration on a bicycle frame

3

Airbrushes

As a starting point, experiment with the airbrush on scrap paper. Vary the paint and air controls and the distance of the airbrush from the work. To spray lines you will need to have the airbrush close to the paper. If you move further away, the band of spray will become broader. Use smooth movements to produce an even colour.

MASKS

A mask is used like a stencil and controls the area of spray on the paper. Frisket film is a clear, low-tack film that is specially made for airbrushing. A cheaper method of masking is to use thin card. Once the stencil has been cut it can be weighted down so that it does not move. Low-tack masking tape and newspaper can be used for simple drawings.

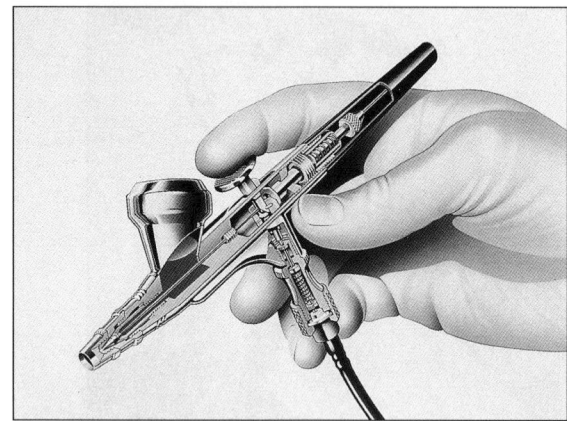

An 'airbrushed' illustration of an airbrush

- Draw the outline lightly onto stretched paper or board (see page 85).

- Plan your colouring stages and how the masks will be used. Dark colours should be sprayed first.

- Mask off all the drawing, exposing only the area to be sprayed. This may then be covered and another part exposed.

- You may wish to leave it open to receive more coats of spray in order to build up a darker tone of colour.

- Details can be added later. Use gouache or paint for bright highlights or to sharpen up blurred edges.

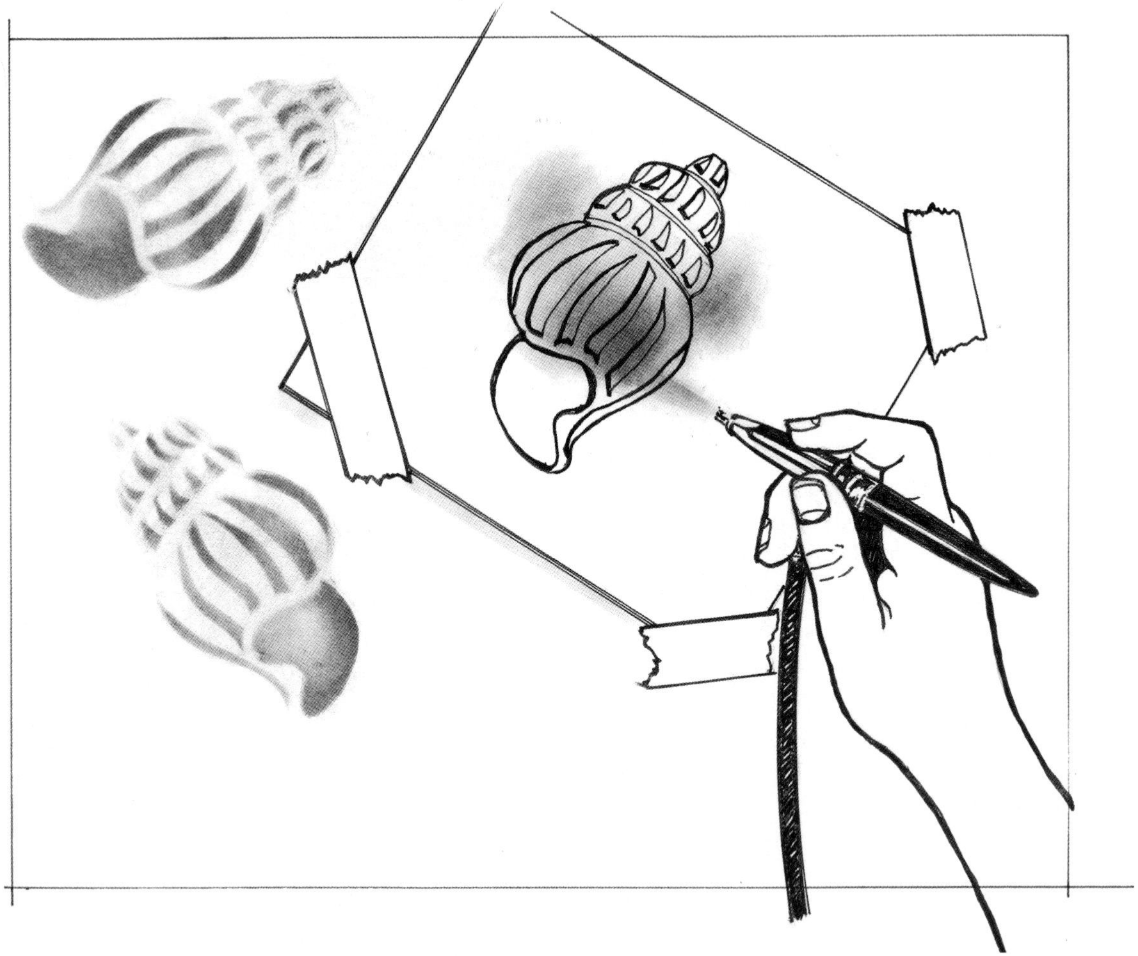

Water-based paints, such as **water colours** and **gouache**, were once the most popular materials for colouring design drawings. They have largely been replaced by markers because these are more convenient to use. Paints do, however, have a special quality and character of their own and should not be neglected. They tend to have a more natural or subtle effect that is desirable for certain subjects.

HOW TO STRETCH PAPER

When working with water-soluble paints or crayons, you will need to use a heavy duty paper that can withstand moisture. Thinner papers tend to buckle and warp when you apply water to them. Alternatively, you can 'stretch' paper onto a board to create a flat, stable surface to work on.

- Soak the paper until it is thoroughly wet. You may use a sponge or carefully float it in a sink of water.

- Drain off the surplus water.

- Lay the paper flat on a clean drawing board.

- Stick it down with gummed paper.

- Allow it to dry.

- Cut the paper off the board with a scalpel or modelling knife when you have finished your painting.

Water-colour Paint

These paints are available in blocks, tubes or bottles. The blocks are probably the most long-lasting and economical to use. Water colour is usually applied to the paper as a thin transparent 'wash' of colour over the top of a pencil or waterproof pen drawing.

As they are transparent, you can lighten a colour by adding more water to the paint to thin the colour down. This allows the white of the paper to shine through giving a paler colour. It is not a good idea to add white to water colours as this tends to make them opaque and the colours become murky.

TO PRODUCE A FLAT WASH OF COLOUR

- Stretch the paper on a board and allow to dry.
- Mix up enough thin paint to cover the area.
- Dampen the paper with a large flat soft brush or sponge.
- Hold the board at a steep angle.
- Charge the brush with enough paint and start working from left to right and down the page.
- Continue working with broad, horizontal strokes to the bottom of the page. Any excess paint should collect at the bottom of the paper and can be mopped up with a tissue or dry brush.
- Do not add pencil or crayon to this drawing until the paper is completely dry or you will damage the surface.

1

2

Fig. 1 Border designs for a plant package

Fig. 2 Fashion drawing

3

These are generally available in tubes or pots and are in paste form. They are similar to water colours but have white added which causes them to lose their transparency. As they have greater covering power, the paint colour is stronger and requires a different painting technique. This type of paint can give strong vibrant colour and is particularly useful for working on coloured backgrounds. It is also suitable for painting areas of flat dense colour.

Gouache needs to be mixed with a small amount of water to make it into an easily-controllable creamy liquid. Apply it to the paper with a soft brush made from animal hair or nylon. If you are only painting a small area and the paper is of good quality, it is not necessary to stretch the paper. If in doubt, test the paint on some spare paper to check that it does not wrinkle.

Point-of-sale display

Presentation visual for seeds packaging

The backgrounds in these presentation drawings help to show off the designs to their best advantage.

Some of the presentation visuals have been given a background scene. This helps to show where the design might be used and, in some cases, to show what the design is. Showing the design used in context in this way can help the design proposal look more convincing. It is even possible to make a design seem more exciting by setting it in an exotic background that hints at a glamorous lifestyle.

The figures placed in a presentation drawing not only suggest *how* the product is used but can give a clear idea of **scale** and **proportion**. Often a simple outline of a figure will give enough information about the size and function of a design and will not over complicate the drawing. If you find these difficult to draw you can make this easier by tracing over images from magazine pictures.

Obviously if the design is intended to be worn, the figure drawing will need to show more detail. It may suggest how the design fits realistically on the body or, in the case of fashion drawings, the figure may be exaggerated to communicate a mood or image.

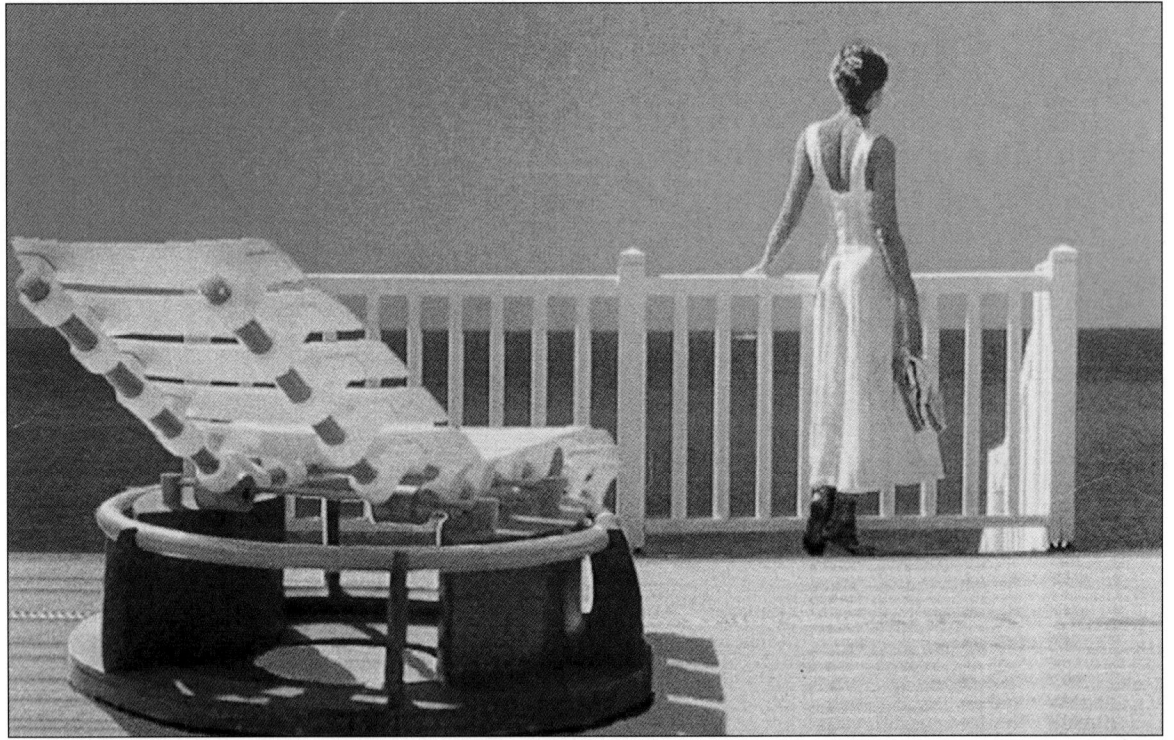

A rotating sun lounger set in an attractive sunny background scene

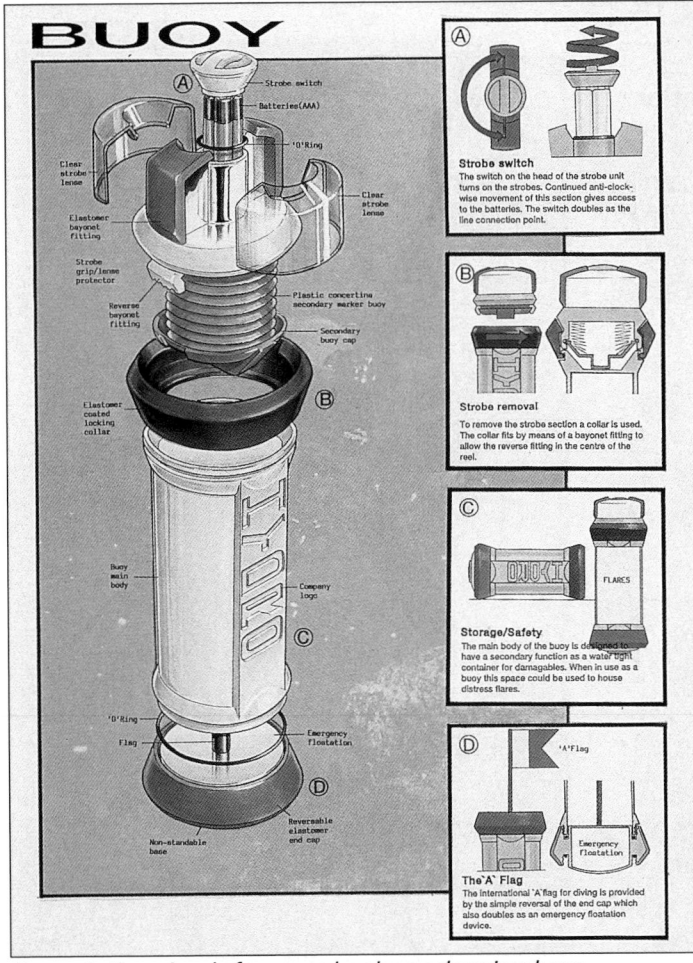

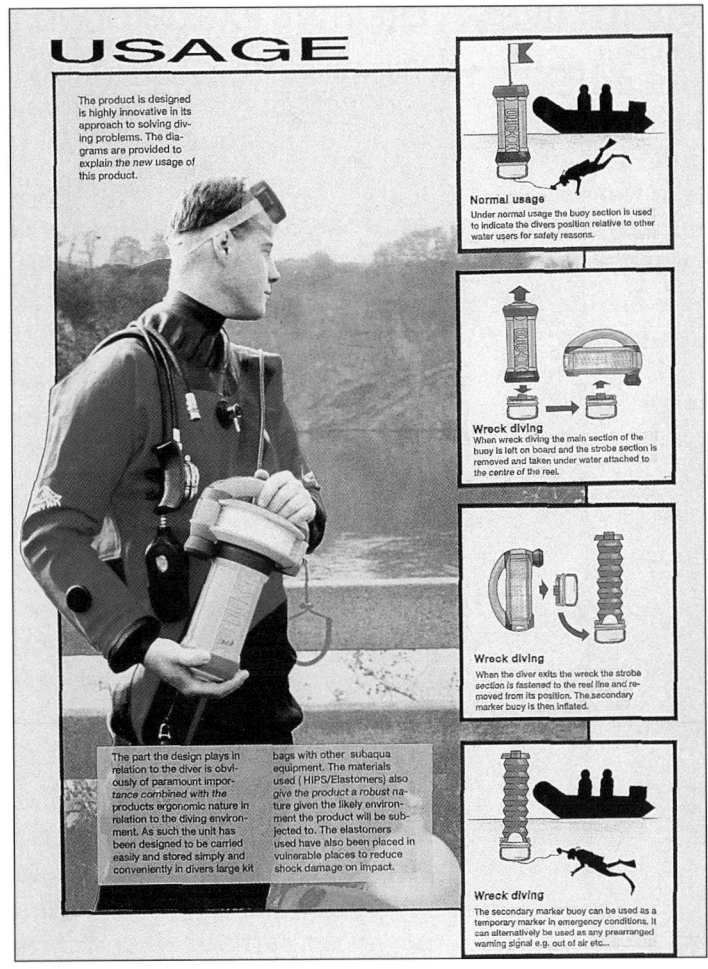

Presentation visuals for a marker buoy showing how and where it is used

If a design proposal is complex, either in terms of components or function, a useful way of conveying information is to show several views of the design on one large drawing. A central pictorial view of the design will indicate what the design *looks* like, while extra views such as cross-sections, magnifications or contexts will communicate *how* it works and *where* it is used.

Notes and diagrams can further support the information about a design proposal but it is important that they are clear and precise. Sensitive use of colour, images, lettering and annotation can work together to enhance design drawings. However, be careful not to overdo it! It is easy to overpower the subject of your drawing with riotous colour, too much information and flashy background techniques.

Background Colour

Background colour can be used to attract the eye and focus it on the object in the drawing. You can use colours that are similar to, and compliment, a particular shade used on an object. Alternatively, contrasting colour will make the design stand out and look dynamic. Where the colour is used to suggest a background shadow or frame, the whole picture gains depth and an added 3D quality.

CREATING BACKGROUND EFFECTS

You can create soft, cloud-like backgrounds with aerosol spray paint or by using an airbrush.

If you require a speckled effect, this can be achieved with a **diffuser** and inks. The diffuser is operated by blowing and is easy to use once you find the correct angle to work at.

A simple way to produce a spattered background is by using a toothbrush with paint such as gouache. Dip the toothbrush into the paint and draw a knife across the bristles to flick a spray of paint onto a surface.

If you want to control the area of spray or produce a sharp edge on your work you will need to use a mask (see page 84).

A simple yet effective finish can be created using a gradually-fading tone of one colour. Gradated coloured papers are available from art shops and stationers, or you can make your own using powdered soft pastels and cotton wool (see page 75) or a spray technique.

Colour-photocopied images from magazines can create realistic settings

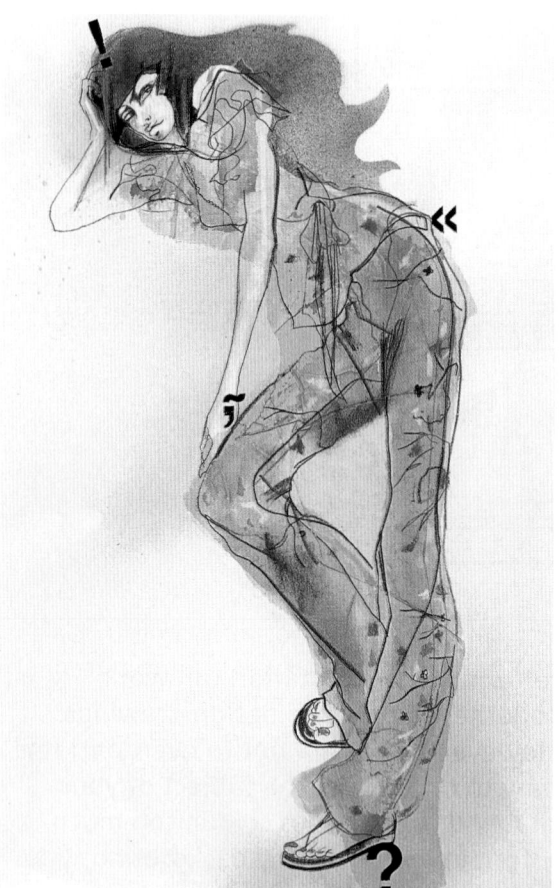

Spray and spatter techniques used on hair and background

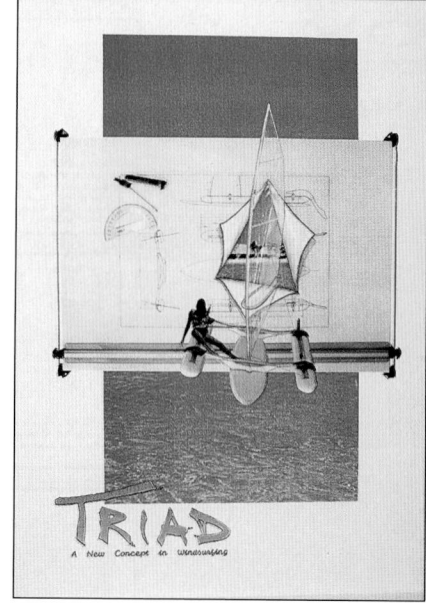

Colour photocopied sea, girl and drawing board

A drawing in collage form, assembled on a gradated background

Background Colour

A PHOTOGRAPHIC BACKGROUND

A suitable photograph or magazine picture can be used as a realistic backdrop for your design. If the picture is too strong and threatens to overpower your drawing, you can tone it down by mounting a sheet of tracing paper over the top. If you decide to make a colour photocopy of the original picture, the strength of the image can be reduced at the printing stage. It is also possible to create unusual and interesting effects by changing the colour range on the copier.

Trimaran with photographic background of water

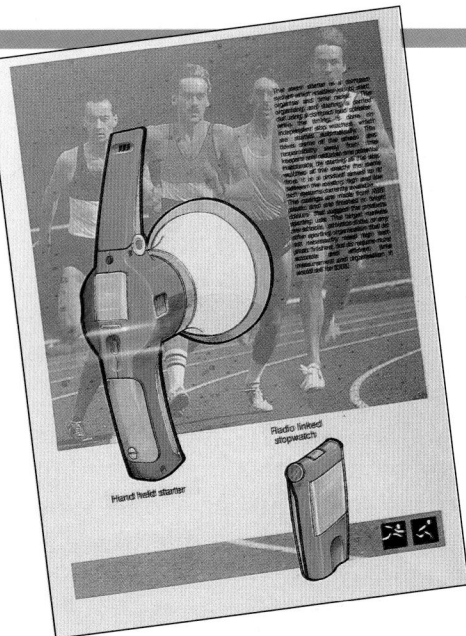

Event starter with sporting background, overlayed with tracing paper

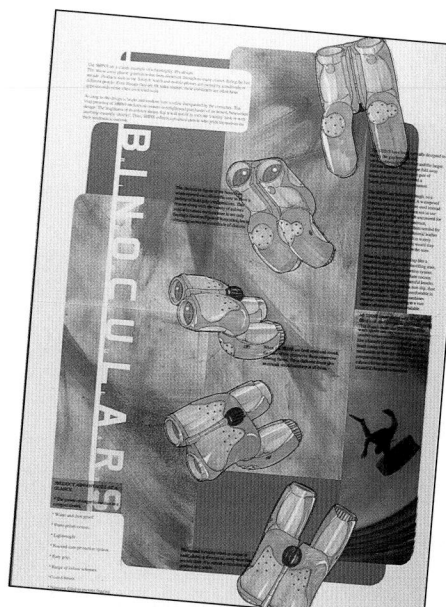

Water-resistant binoculars. The sea effect background was produced with pastel and lighter fluid

Studio markers worked in a sketchy, relaxed way can create the dynamic backgrounds often found on car design drawings. A similar effect can be achieved using powdered soft pastels and cotton wool soaked in a solvent such as lighter fluid. Dip the damp cotton wool in the powdered colour and make broad confident strokes across the paper. Use a clean side of the cotton wool for each new colour.

Car mounted on background of pastel and lighter fluid

These techniques are more effective if they are given a sharp, neat edge. You can do this either by masking the area with tape or by cutting out the background with a modelling knife. It can be mounted onto the presentation drawing using spray adhesive.

Painting Models

The quality of finish applied to presentation models is important if they are to look realistic. One of the most convenient ways to produce a good paint finish is to use cans of spray paint. They come in a wide variety of colours and are simple to apply.

Before spraying it is important that the surface of the model is free from defects. Although a surface blemish may look small prior to painting, the finish will tend to make it stand out.

Make sure that the surface has been finished smoothly with fine sand paper to remove any defects.

The first stage in finishing a timber-based model is to give it a coat of sanding sealer. This can be applied with a brush and will seal the surface. When dry, it should be lightly rubbed down with a fine abrasive paper. This will provide a base surface for the paint. An additional coat of sealer can be applied if necessary (Fig. 1).

Next, apply a coat of primer. It is better to cover the model with a number of light coats rather than one heavy one. When this is dry, you should be able to see any defects more clearly. To get rid of these, use a fine surface filler and then cut it back with a fine abrasive paper. A further coat of primer can then be applied (Fig. 2).

Finally, when you are satisfied with the quality of the surface, you can start to build up the finishing coat of paint. You may need to use two to three coats of paint to achieve a professional quality (Fig. 3).

Models made in plastic can be finished in a similar way. Initially the surface of the model should be lightly abraded to give the paint a 'key'. This time, use a plastics primer as the first coat. From this point the finishing process is the same as for timber-based models.

Metal models are initially given a coat of metal etch primer.

1

2

3

In the world of mass production, many products are injection-moulded and include details that rise above or sink below the surface. In creating a realistic model of a chosen design, we can represent details, such as lettering or surface texture, by being inventive in our use of materials.

Lettering is an important part of product identity. It can be used as part of the moulding process or it can be printed on after the component has been manufactured.

To simulate text on a product model, it is important that a professional appearance is obtained. Commercially-available self-adhesive lettering is a useful method of applying some surface detail. Although the paper is quite thin, the letters will show up in relief when the model is given a spray-paint finish. Alternatively, personalised text can be created by drawing onto self-adhesive address labels and then cutting them out accurately with a sharp knife. If one thickness of paper does not give sufficient relief then it can be built up with extra layers prior to cutting out the letters. This will make the text stand out more on the finished product.

For lettering that appears to be printed onto the product, the best type to use is **dry transfer lettering**. This gives a professional appearance and is quite easy to use. It is important that you use a style of lettering that is appropriate to the image of the product.

You can also design your own lettering or logo. Draw it out on a dry transfer sheet and then apply it to your work.

Self-adhesive lettering

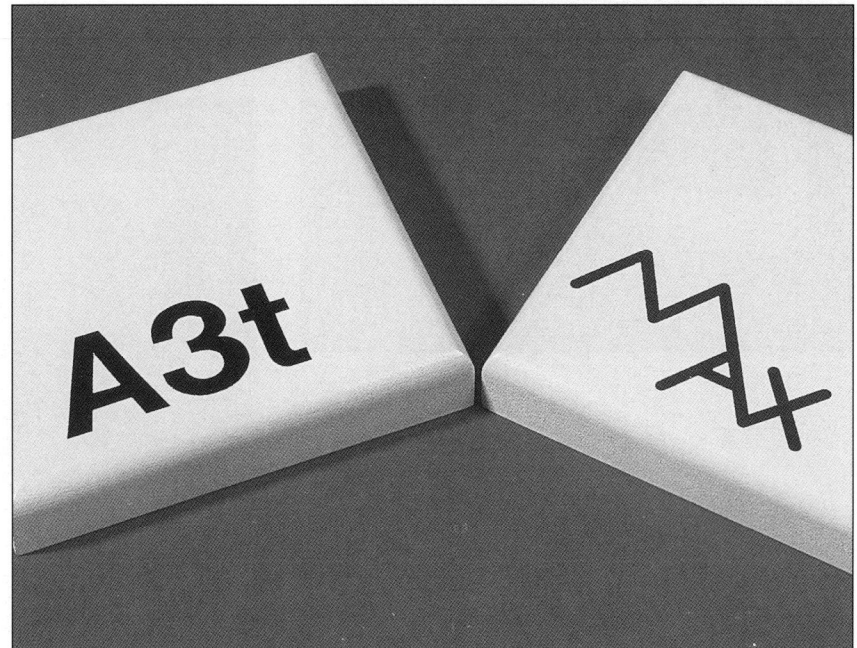

Dry transfer lettering

Modelling Details

There are many ways in which realistic finishes can be simulated using a wide variety of everyday materials. It is important to use your imagination to achieve an end result that creates an effective model. Listed below are a range of ideas for producing convincing finishes.

Textures can be created by applying wet and dry abrasive paper to a model. This is useful for products that have to be gripped. This type of surface is often seen in injection-moulded products. Cut out the shape required and then glue it in position. When the model is sprayed with paint, the texture blends into the surface.

Fabrics such as cotton can be stuck to a timber base and then sprayed with aluminium paint to simulate a metal casting.

Rubberised paint is available which can be applied to a timber or MDF base by brushing. This will give the impression of a rubber model or component.

A range of pastes are available that come in different finishes, some metallic such as brass and copper. These can be applied to almost any base material and when polished give the impression of a metal product.

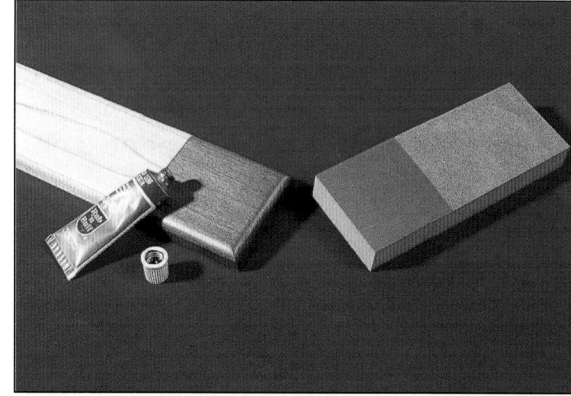

When making architectural models, concrete can be simulated by mixing sand with PVA wood glue. When set, it will give a realistic impression of the building material.

Components of the same form can be replicated in a similar way by making one of them and then taking a **mould** from it. This mould can be made by either vacuum forming, using silicone, plaster or casting sand. When the mould has been created, it can be filled with car-body filler or casting resin to make the component. Many components can be taken off a single mould.

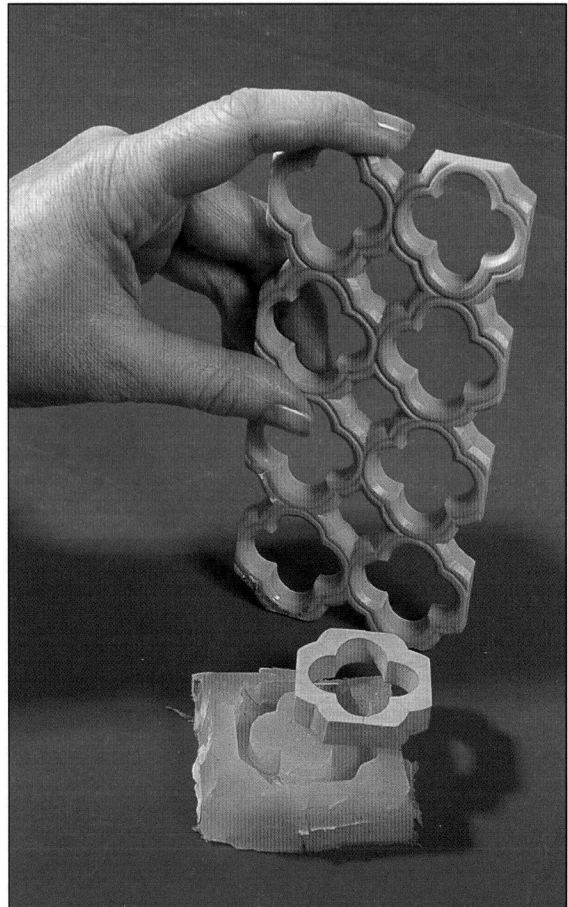

Silicone moulds can be taken from components and then filled with resin to create replicas of the original.

Foam can be stuck underneath buttons to simulate the effect of it working when pressed.

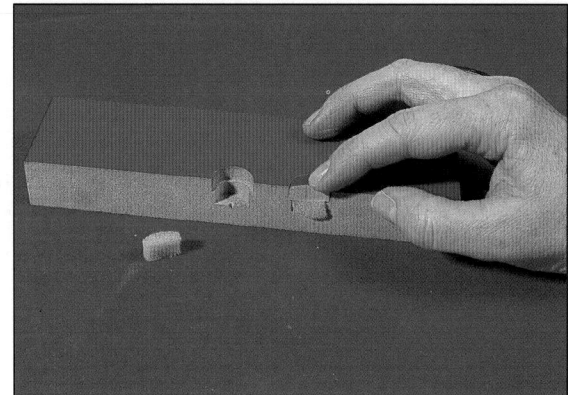

A range of everyday objects and materials can be used either directly onto a solid block model or on a mould which is then used in vacuum forming.

Small buttons can be made from sweets or pills.

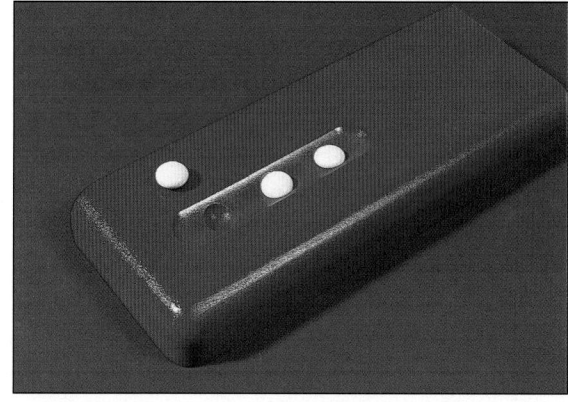

Wire and string can be applied to models to achieve a ribbed effect.

Modelling Details

There are a range of techniques which can be used to make presentation models more realistic and easier to produce. Here are a few ideas which may help in their production.

It can be difficult to simulate the split line, which is often seen at the join of two injection-moulded components. This is sometimes needed when joining two vacuum-formed components. To make the process simple, you can use a double vacuum forming. Having made the mould and vacuum formed over it, the process can be repeated to give a double skin. When the edges of these formings are trimmed to size, they can be staggered to produce positive and negative locators.

In solid block models, the same problem will be encountered. In this case, roughly cut out a recess around the area where the line will be and then fill it in with car-body filler. Before the filler sets, press in the edge of a plastic sheet, such as acrylic. When the filler is set, the plastic sheet will pull out to leave a split line. This can be done in stages if necessary, starting with a short length and then using the ends of the formed line as a guide to locate the plastic sheet for the next section.

A similar method can be used to make internal shapes. It is far easier to make a positive component than a negative one. Take, for example, an elliptical recess into which a button or switch is to be set. Rather than have to gouge out the recess, cut its male equivalent in acrylic and give it a polished finish. A hole larger than the size of the recess can be cut in the model and filled with car-body filler. Before it sets, press in your acrylic component then allow the filler to set to give the required recess.

Indented lettering can be produced in the same way.

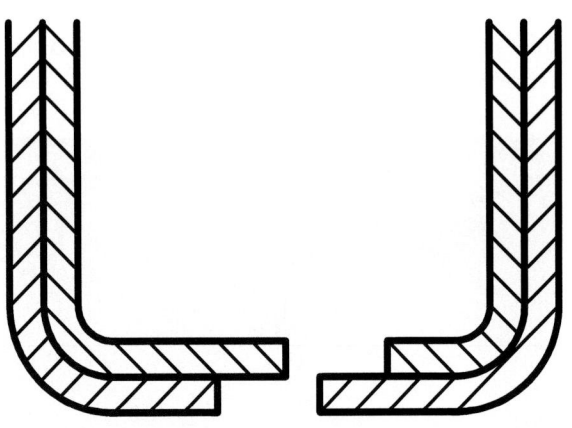
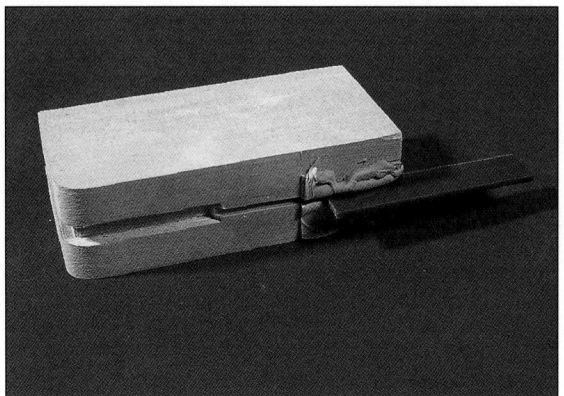
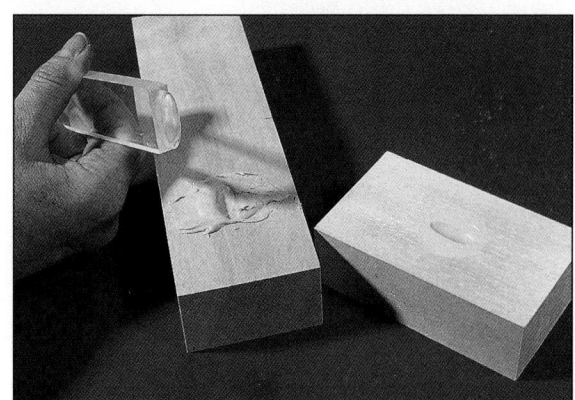

Spirit-based markers can be used on aluminium to simulate an anodised finish.

You can make simple springs by winding thin wire around a rod or dowel. When using a metal such as aluminium, it will slightly work-harden as it is being coiled and so provide some springiness.

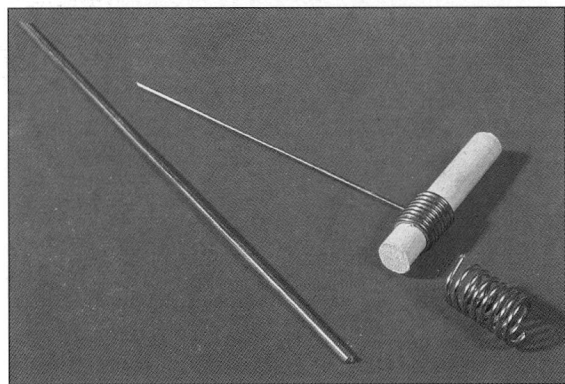

Clear acrylic is a useful material for simulating glass/plastic lenses and digital displays. The gentle dome of a lens can be turned on either the metal or wood lathe using conventional tools. Wet and dry abrasive paper followed by a polishing material can then be used to finish the acrylic.

Other shapes can be made in the same way but will clearly be more labour intensive depending on their complexity.

Computer graphics and/or text can be set behind the acrylic component to give a more realistic impression of the finished product.

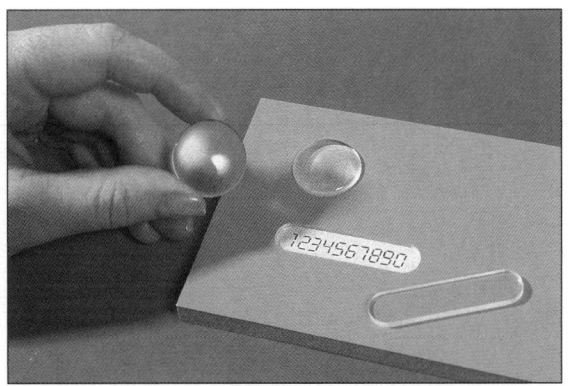

When making scale models, it is simple to give the impression of the actual material using reduced photocopies on acetate sheet. Images of materials, such as perforated sheet steel, can be found in trade magazines. These can be reduced and applied to your model using spray mount.

2D CAD Rendering

The more sophisticated graphics software can produce high quality images (using up to 16 million colours!). This is an ideal way of producing realistic models, giving a photographic quality to your work.

As well as the model being given a solid block of colour to simulate a matt paint finish, surface decoration and textures can be applied. These options can be used to represent, in a more realistic way, the actual materials that the finished object will be made of. This type of computer modelling is ideal for presenting ideas where a three-dimensional model has not been produced. You can also experiment with different colour ranges with these systems.

Bathroom layout

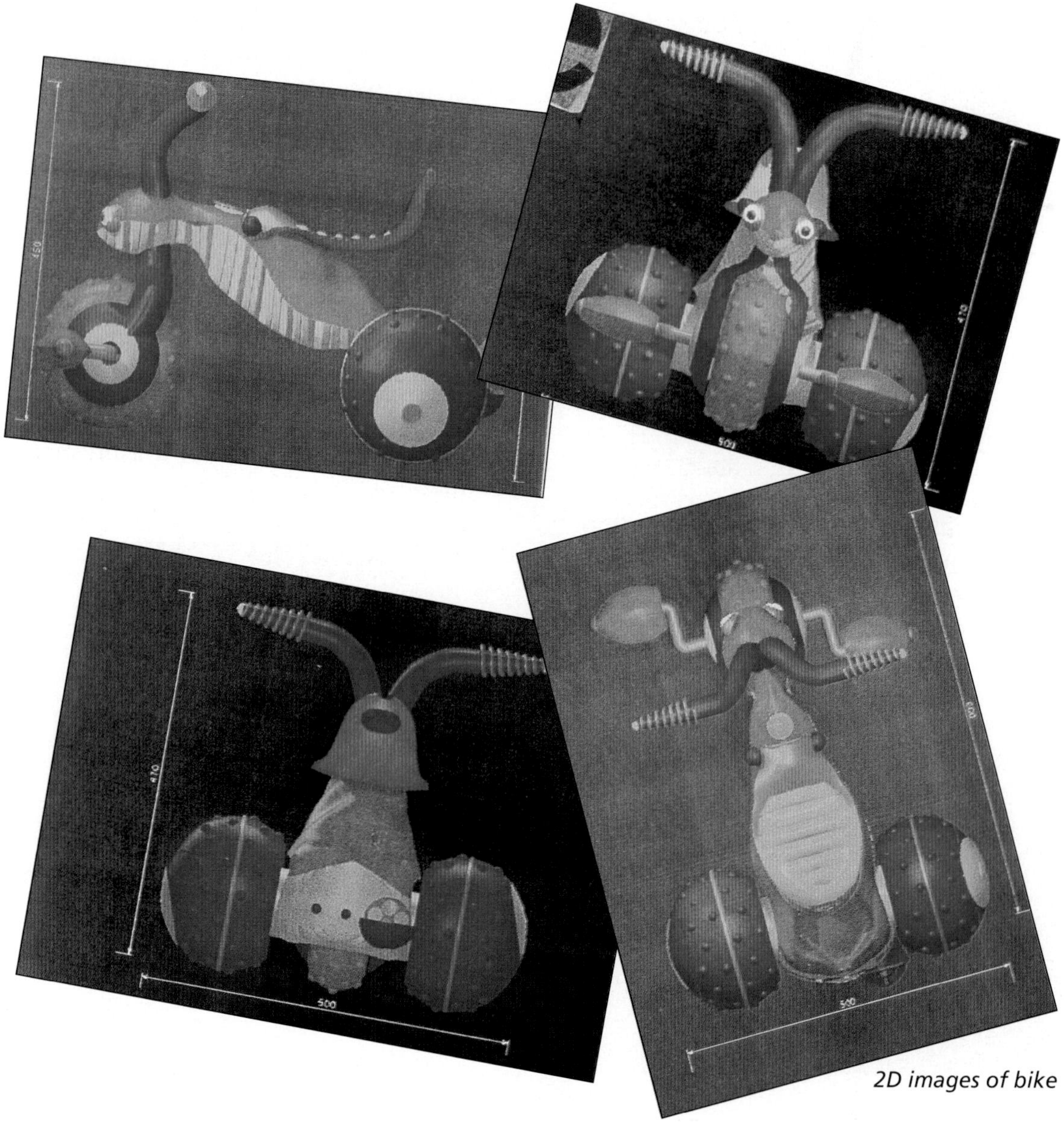

2D images of bike

Three-dimensional modelling software can also be used to present design ideas. The advantage they have over 2D CAD packages is that when a model has been produced, the view can be changed so that any side, part or detail can be seen to give a clearer impression of the design. If interior or architectural models are being produced, the user can 'walk' into the spaces to gain a clearer impression of room layout.

Again, colour variations can be made to show how the model will look with different combinations.

Stereolithography

Although this process is an industrial one, it is useful to know how modelling techniques are developing in conjunction with computer aided design.

The advantage of this system is that it overcomes the expensive and time-consuming process usually associated with prototype manufacture. In basic terms, it works in a similar way to laser printing. In the same way that your computer controls a laser to send ink to the paper, in **stereolithography** the computer directs a laser over a tank of liquid photopolymer (a light sensitive plastic). At the point where the laser beam touches the liquid, it solidifies to give a fine layer of the model (0.1 mm).

Using computer aided design, a three-dimensional image is created and then 'sliced' into a series of layers that build up to make the model. Each layer is then directed to the stereolithography equipment, one after the other. The model is constructed on a movable platform which will descend by the thickness of a layer after it has been created. The layers are constructed, one on top of the other, to gradually build up the three-dimensional form.

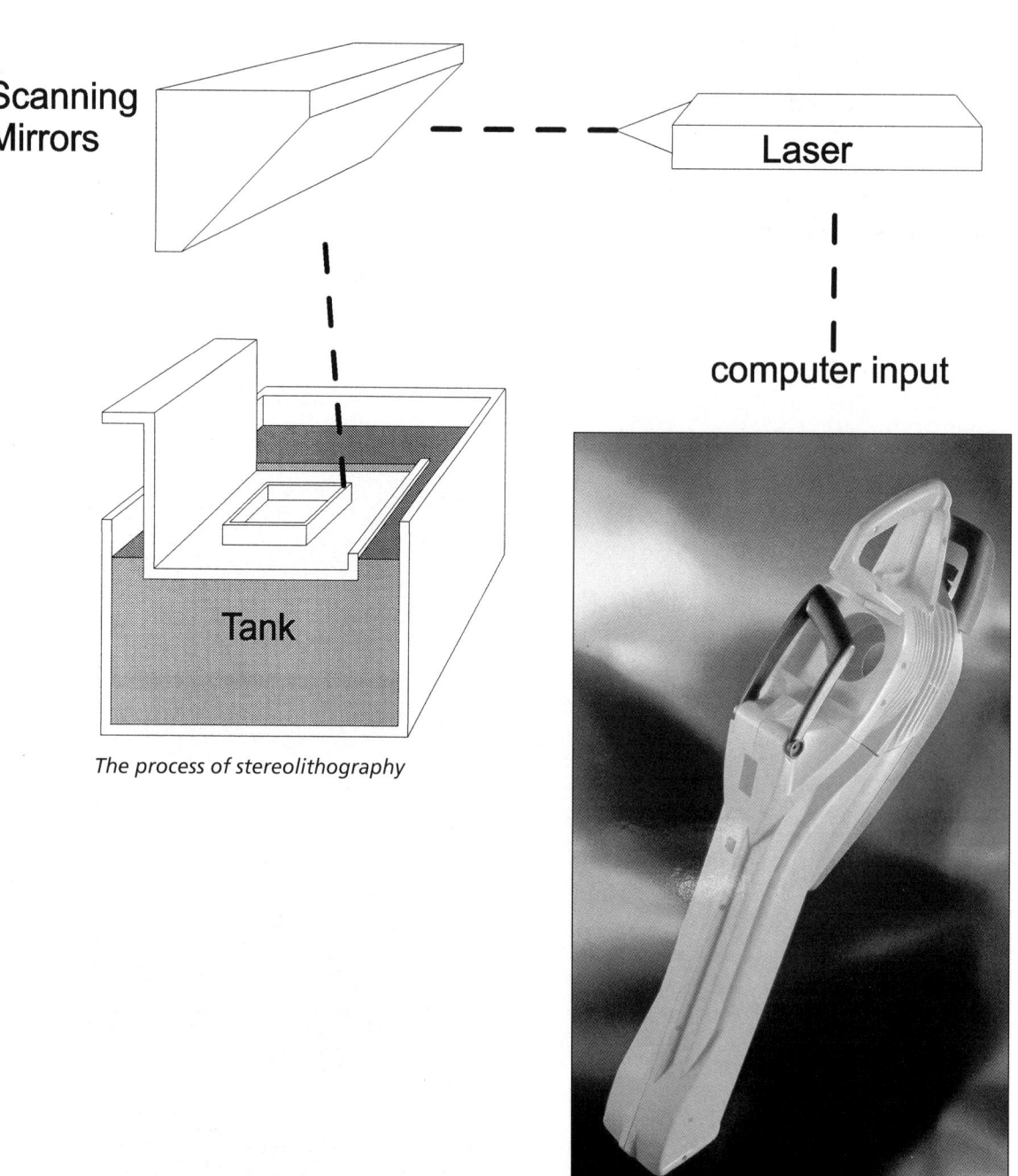

Scanning Mirrors

Laser

computer input

Tank

The process of stereolithography

'Flymo' model produced through stereolithography

Jaguar's acclaimed *XK8*, produced in 1996, combines automotive craftsmanship and dramatic styling. Initial drawings were started in 1991, but a further 5 years of research and development work followed with meticulous attention given to every design detail.

The following pages highlight some of the modelling techniques that were used by the team of engineers and designers involved in developing the concept and getting the car into production.

These full-scale clay models show different versions of the facia/instrument panel and layout of controls. Details have been added with simple mock-ups of components and materials allowing for judgements to be made about the appearance and ergonomics involved.

Each model has been given a specific theme and identity, some of which are in complete contrast, for example 'traditional' and 'avant-garde'. Public response and reaction to these models provided important feedback for the design team.

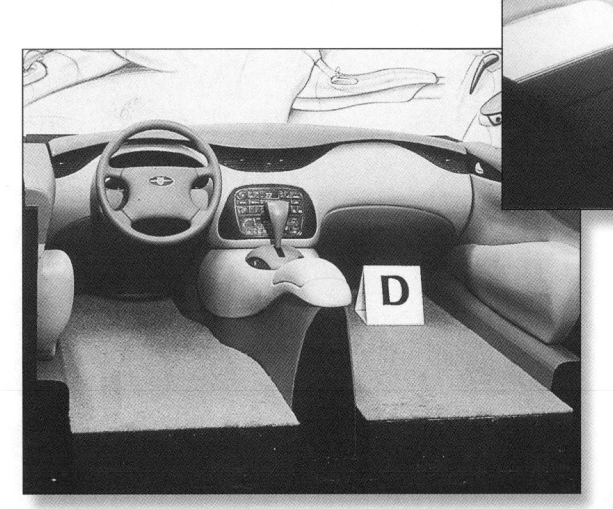

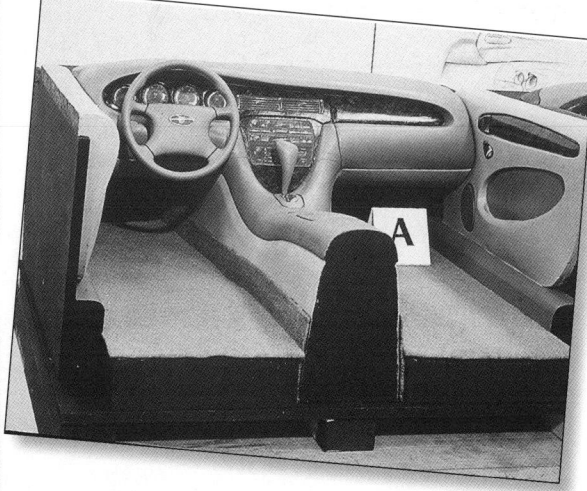

Case Study: Jaguar *XK8*

The modelling processes used to develop the shell of the *XK8* and subsequent performance testing are many and include: styling, ergonomics, safety, performance in road conditions and electronics. The aerodynamic style, a distinct feature of the Jaguar, was developed using:

- 2D presentation drawings in marker and pastel
- full-size clay models made with the use of CNC technology
- full-size facsimile models to simulate the finished product.

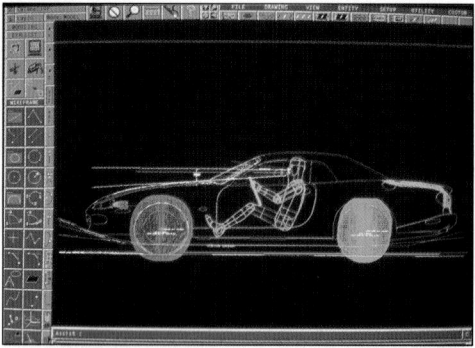

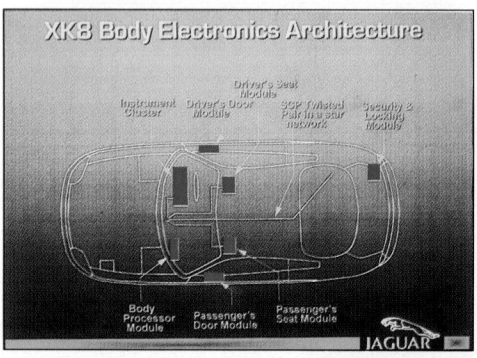

Ergonomic considerations included:

- the seating position and the related field of vision of the driver, evaluated through the use of CAD
- the location of the many electronic components and their accessibility through CAD simulation.

Various tests had to be carried out and included:

- crash-test simulation through CAD which looked at the forces applied to the car in a collision

- a full-size 'environmental cube' made to exact specification. Basically this is the shell of the *XK8* which was then used to determine the fit of all other components prior to production

- a test rig was built to simulate road conditions and check durability

- full-size working prototypes were made to carry out various performance tests e.g.: how the car will behave in wet conditions.

When all aspects of the car had been modelled and tested, the coupé and convertible went into production and were launched on the world-wide market.

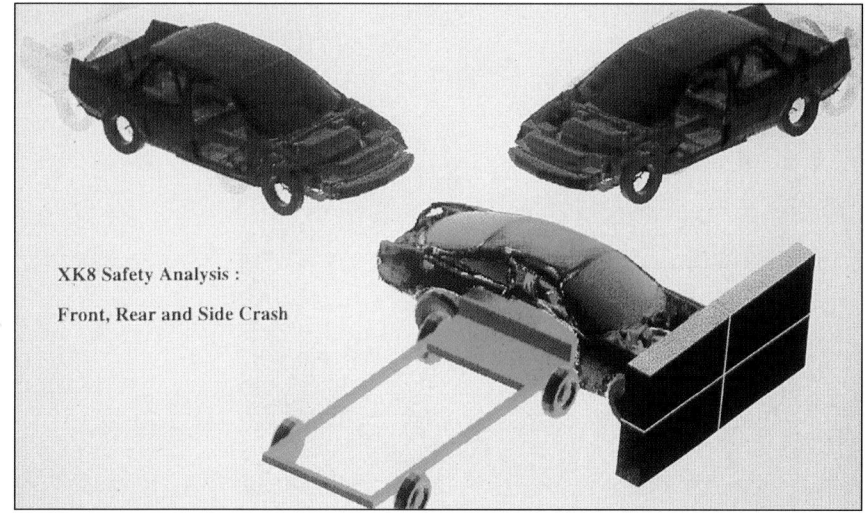

XK8 Safety Analysis :

Front, Rear and Side Crash

Case Study: Chair

JOHN BAIRSTOW: DESIGNER/MAKER

Many different factors have to be considered when designing a chair. It must:

- be comfortable to sit on
- give support to the back
- be structurally sound
- be visually effective.

An initial brief gave the design certain restrictions:

- The chair should be designed so that its basic form (the frame) could be adapted for a range of products.
- A jointing method should be used that has decorative/structural qualities.
- A system of 'flat-packing' the chair should be built in.

Modelling Processes:

- Following initial sketching, a number of fifth-scale models were made in card. These considered visual quality along with general structure.
- Full-scale corner details were made. These considered component size, constructional/aesthetic qualities and combination of materials.
- A realistic scale model gave a clearer impression of the finished product.
- A full-size mock-up determined seating position in relation to back and arm support.

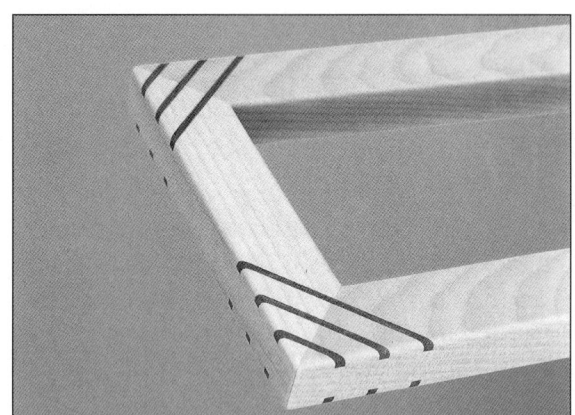

ROBERT BARBER: DESIGNER

This piece of furniture was produced for an exhibition and was therefore intended to attract attention rather than be comfortable to live with. Its appearance was developed from an interest in modern 'high rise' architecture. The materials used – Corian, concrete, plywood and polished steel – reinforced this architectural theme. In this case. Corian was used because it closely resembles the polished granite which is often used in modern architecture.

Modelling Processes:

• Initial ideas were explored through elevation and perspective sketching (Fig. 1).

• The form of the design was developed by making a full-size model. Various changes were made to the model as the design evolved. The materials used are hardboard, MDF, dowel and cardboard tube (Figs. 2 and 3).

• The appearance model also highlighted a number of structural problems. Because of this, a second 'test' model was made in order to develop a more rigid structure. The materials used here are MDF and mild steel rod (Figs. 4 and 5).

• Final decisions about details, such as the drawer pulls and surface finishes, were made by making full-size details of parts of the design.

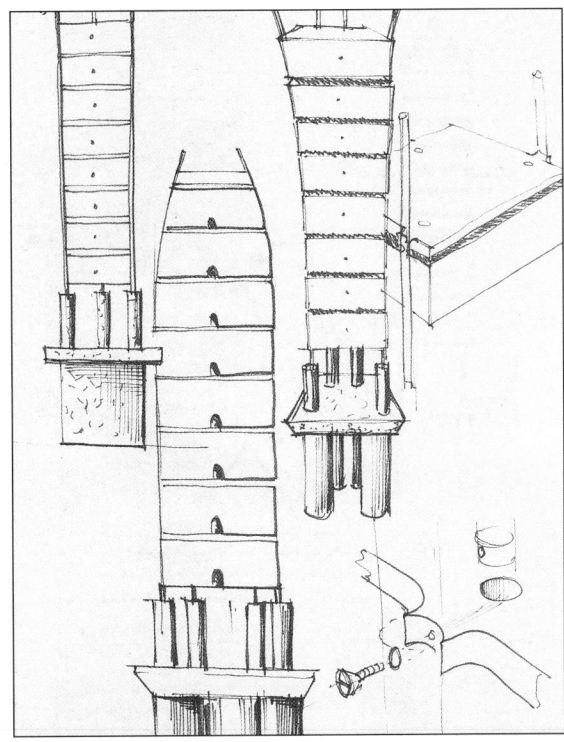

1

4

5

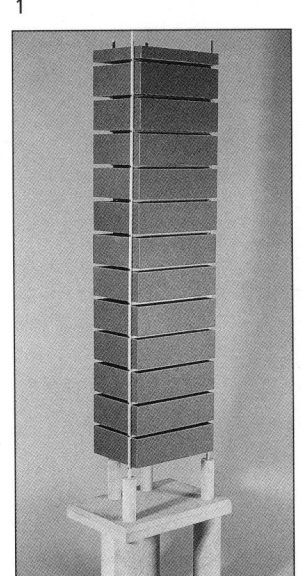

2

3

6

Case Study: Exhibition Design

PHIL MELLOR: EXHIBITION DESIGNER

Linnel, a firm of exhibition contractors, are based in West Yorkshire. Most of their work involves producing stands for exhibitions such as the 'Motor Show'. They regularly design and install them for clients at major venues throughout the UK and Europe.

Pace Electronics required a prestigious exhibition stand which reflected their position as a market leader in the world of satellite and cable television systems. They had committed a large budget to this event, and expected the stand to create a major impact with their customers and competitors.

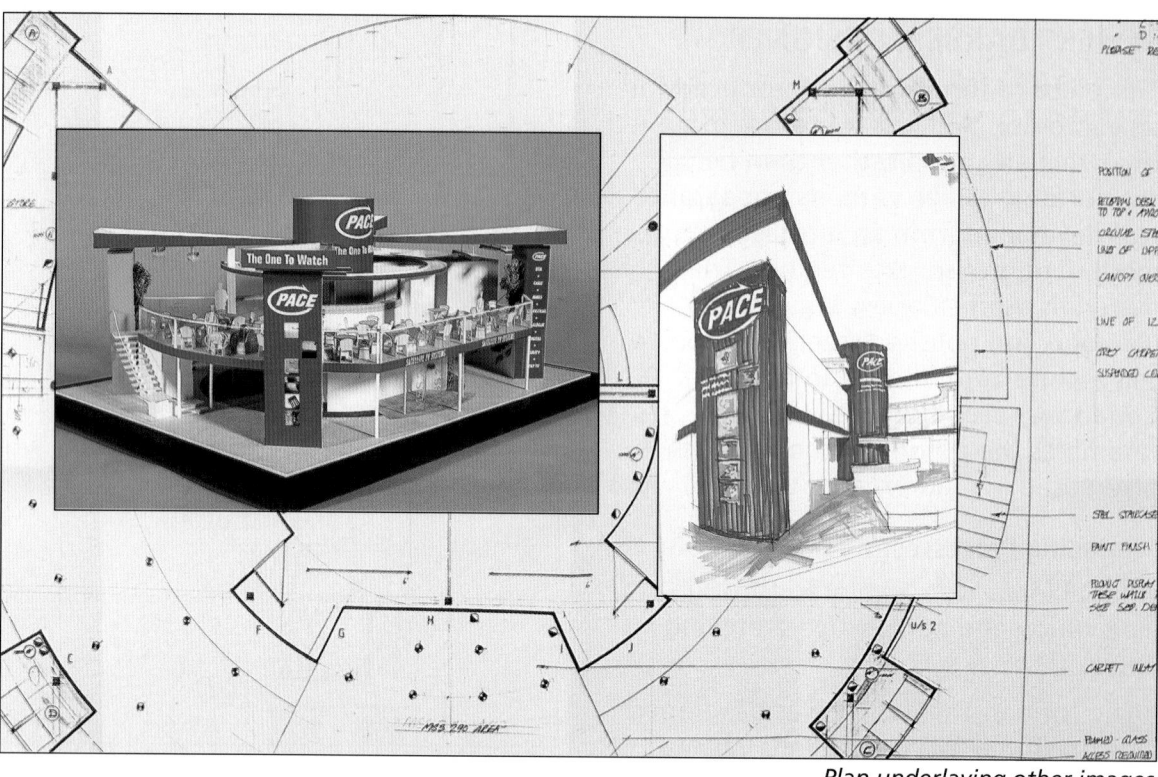

Plan underlaying other images

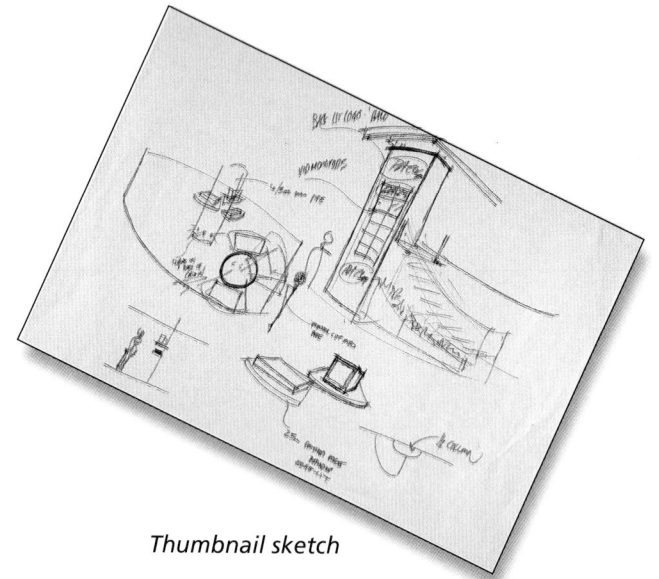

Thumbnail sketch

Modelling Processes

- In briefing discussions, quick thumbnail sketches helped the designer to establish the client's requirements.

- Marker visuals were used to explore initial ideas and discuss colour options.

- When the design had been agreed, detailed plan and elevation drawings were produced.

- Finally, an accurate and detailed scale model was produced. Linnel find this to be one of the most effective ways of helping the client to see what the stand will really look like.

PETER KNIGHT
BA(HONS) INDUSTRIAL DESIGN
SHEFFIELD HALLAM UNIVERSITY

This project was based around the idea that toasting could be a continuous process rather than a single event. Slices of bread are placed on a conveyor and fed through the machine to produce a continuing supply of toast.

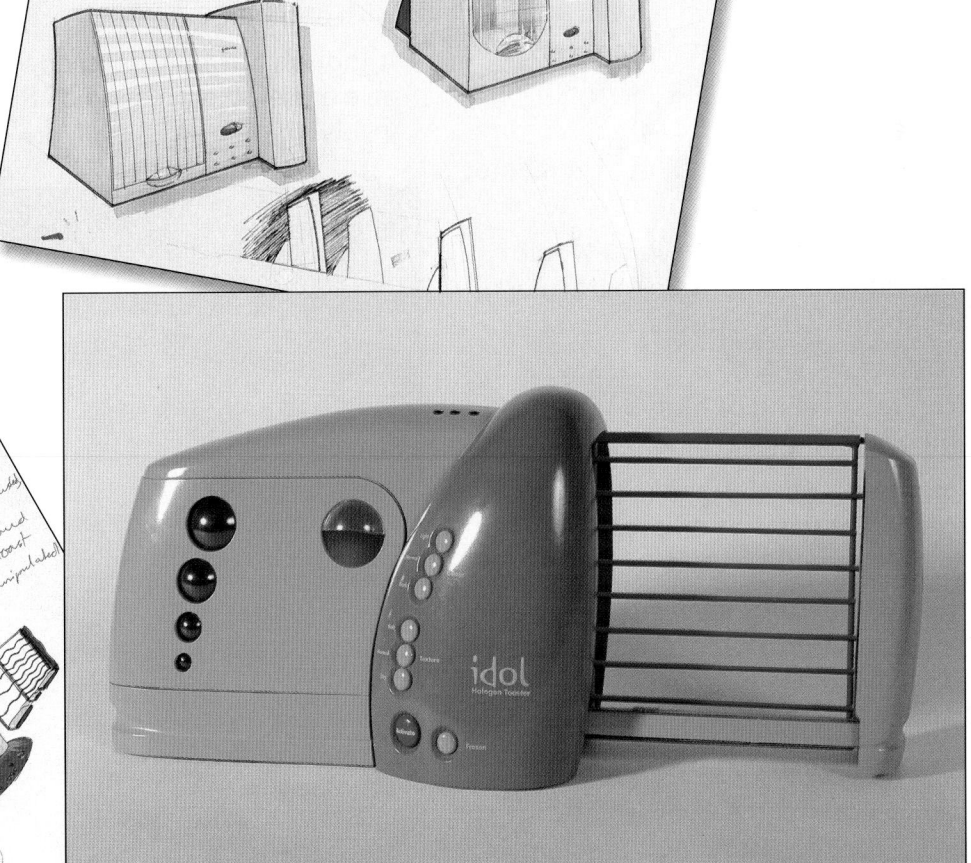

Thumbnails and perspective sketches used to explore initial ideas

MDF model of toaster

Case Study: Packaging for Halfords Motor Oils

PENTAGRAM DESIGN LIMITED

Pentagram is an international design consultancy specialising in product design, architecture and graphic design. Clients include Gillette, Kenwood and British Rail.

The Brief

Halfords' full brief to Pentagram was quite complex. It included the following important aims:

- To increase their share of the UK market for motor oils.

- To have a strong image which would attract customer attention, particularly when the product is displayed on the shelf.

- To create a feeling of high quality, leading to a higher selling price.

- To improve customer understanding of the different types of oil available, and how they should be used.

- To incorporate distinctive advantages over competitors brands, such as ease of pouring and clearer labelling.

- To distinguish Halfords Motor Oils as a superior product.

- To achieve these improvements at no increase in the existing manufacturer's costs.

Modelling Processes

- The initial 'lash-up' gave some idea of the volume and weight of the product. It also explored different handle positions.

- White card models provided a quick and inexpensive way of comparing one idea with another.

- Although not fully detailed, they did give a useful impression of the forms involved.

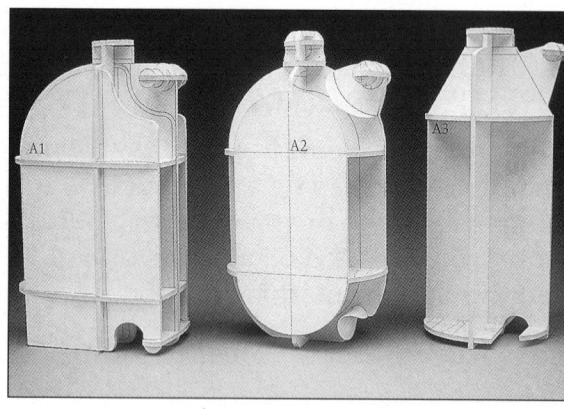

Case Study: Packaging for Halfords Motor Oils

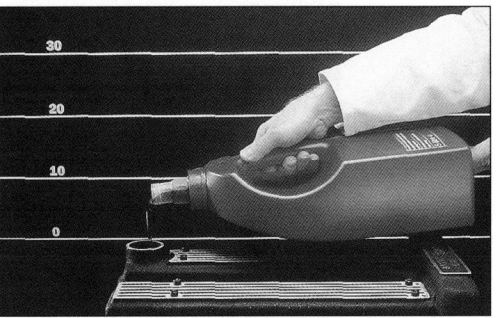

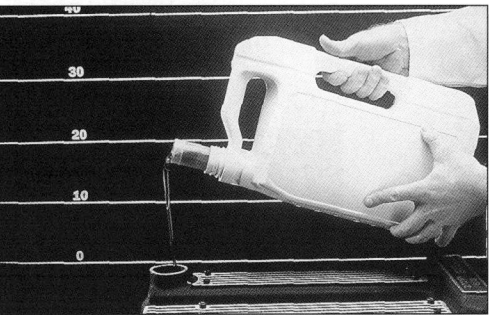

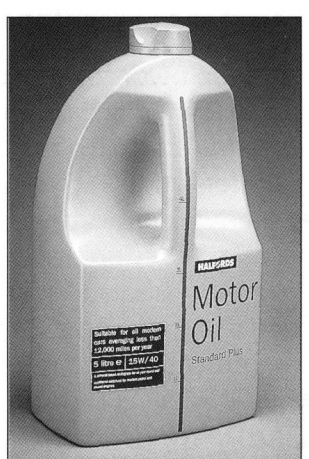

- Accurate foam models were made to work out the finer details of form, and also to test the handling properties of each design.

- A final, detailed appearance model, complete with graphics, was then made to give a better understanding of the product. This model had an accurate weight and was sufficiently realistic to be used for market research.

- The pouring characteristics of the new product are compared with an existing competitor.

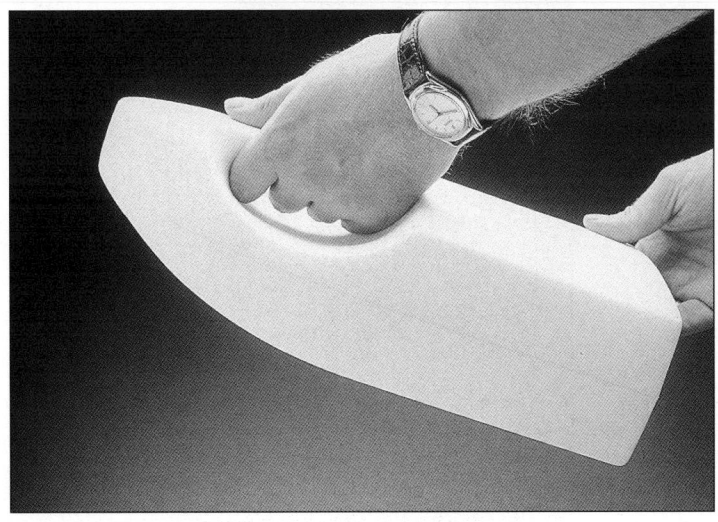

Winner: Design Effectiveness Awards 1996.

International Advertising Awards 1996

Case Study: Dyson Vacuum Cleaner

JAMES DYSON: DESIGNER

James Dyson, the inventor of the *Dual Cycle* vacuum cleaner, is passionate about design. He wants to create better products and feels that it is important that other manufacturers understand the value of using the design process. Often people think that this process is somewhat mysterious and choose to avoid it. The process of design, though, is far from mysterious. As Dyson says, *'design is not about genius. It is about cardboard and sticky tape, borrowing ideas and testing every detail until it works.'*

The development of the Dyson vacuum cleaner demonstrates this very clearly. He 'borrowed' the initial idea from a piece of industrial equipment used to extract dust from factories. This technology had never been applied to a domestic vacuum cleaner before, but he was sure that it could be used to create a more efficient machine. Although the system worked on an industrial scale, he had to build hundreds of models before he was satisfied that he had a working prototype. Further models were then needed to develop the appearance, as well as other details such as structure and ergonomic performance. In all, the design process involved building literally thousands of models. This is what he means when he says, *'testing every detail until it works'*.

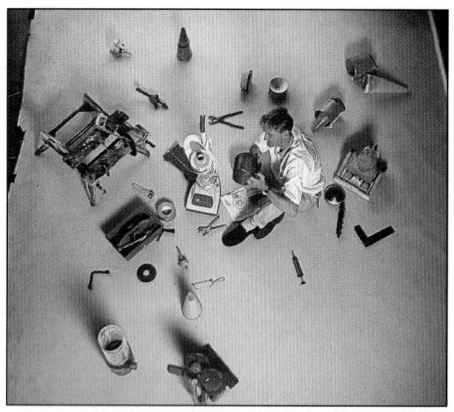
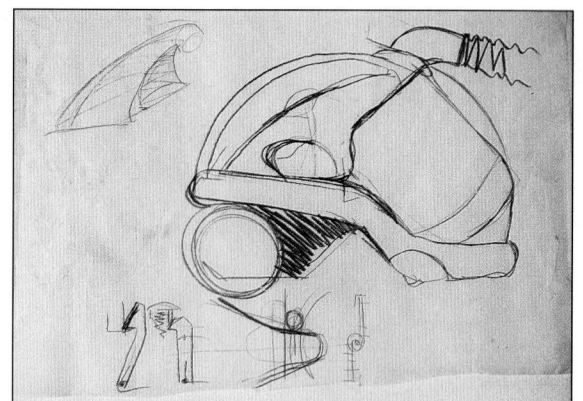

James Dyson working on an early development model

An early prototype

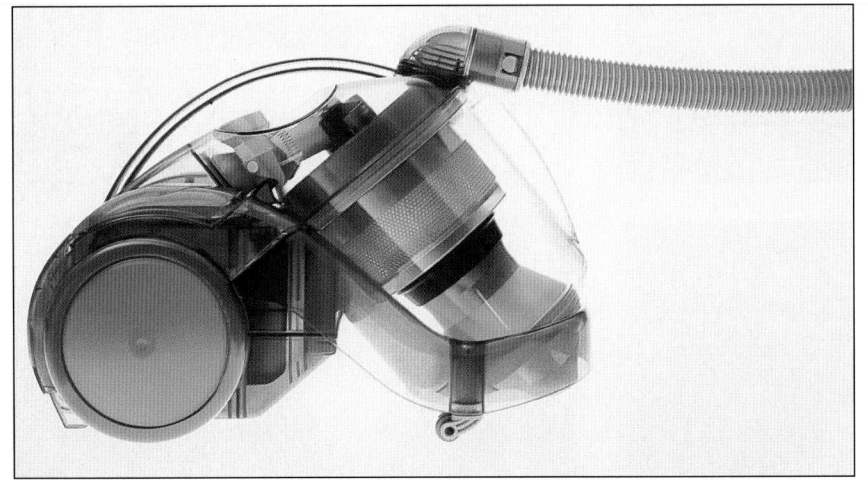

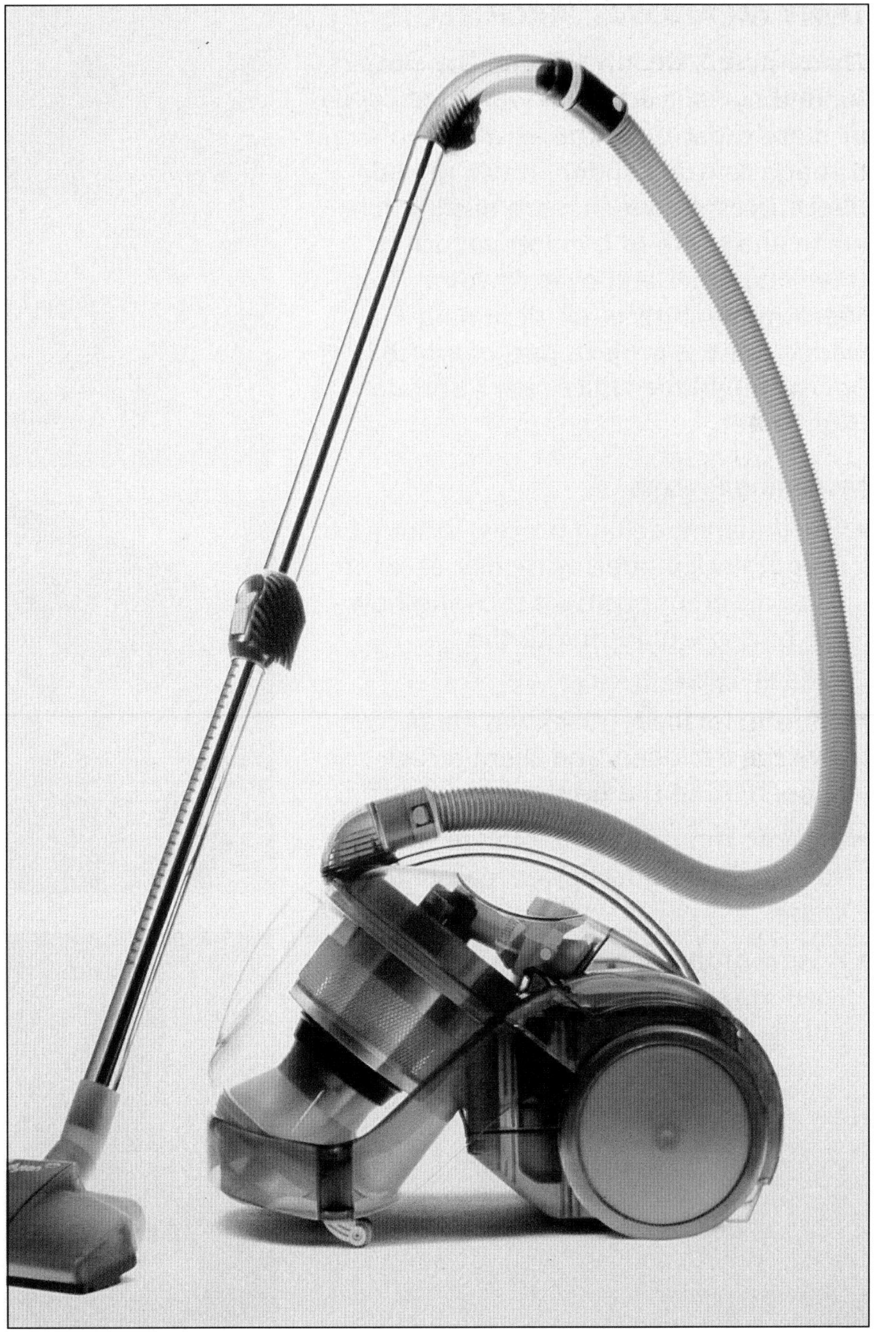

Case Study: Architecture – Thameslink 2000

TONY MEADOWS: ARCHITECTS

Thameslink 2000 is a £580 million project, funded by Railtrack, that will significantly increase capacity on the existing route through central London. It will provide direct access between more destinations north and south of London, reducing travelling times and overcrowding. Tony Meadows Architects are designing a viaduct for the project, part of which is a bowstring bridge which spans Borough High Street.

Modelling Process

- The initial modelling process included rough block models with images taken from different positions showing how the bridge would fit into the surroundings.

- A more detailed model was made to give the designers and client a clear impression of the finished structure.

- A photo montage with models of vehicles and figures gives realism to the scene.

- A view of the bridge taken at street level shows how it will look to the public.

ANTONIO GAUDI: ARCHITECT AND DESIGNER

Antonio Gaudi was a Spanish architect working in Barcelona between 1878 and 1926. His buildings were technically and visually inventive; different from anything seen before. Words such as 'fantastic', 'magical', 'bizarre' and 'exotic' have all been used to describe their visual quality. He was inspired by natural form and this is clearly seen in the visual character of his buildings. He was an engineer as well as an artist, and pioneered new methods of building using concrete and steel.

Gaudi's attention to detail meant that he had to work very closely with the artists and crafts' people who constructed his buildings. Many of his designs were complicated and difficult to explain by drawing. Because of this he developed the technique of using models to explore and communicate his ideas.

Fig. 1
Replicas of the plaster models used by Gaudi

Fig. 3
The modelling technique he developed is still used today in the completion work of the cathedral

Fig. 4
Weights are suspended from strings to form the shape of the arches used within the structure

2

4

1

3

5

Case Study: Diver's Propulsion Unit

JIM DAWSON
BA(HONS) INDUSTRIAL DESIGN
SHEFFIELD HALLAM UNIVERSITY

Jim Dawson was interested in developing a propulsion system for the type of one-man vehicle used by divers to help them move around under water. His intention was to use a larger propeller than normal. This would enable it to turn at a much slower speed, therefore making it safer for the diver. A propeller with the bearings and drive system located around the rim was chosen as the most effective way of achieving this, however this technology had to be tested before it could be included in the design.

Small-scale model

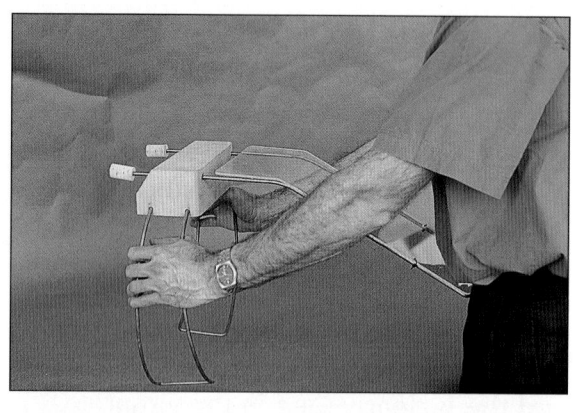

Modelling Process

- A full-size test-rig was built after experiments with small-scale working models. A design engineer assisted with the shape, angle and number of blades required for the annular propeller.

- The rig was taken to a test tank to find out whether the theory would work in practice.

- Many other development models were built, including one which was used in the swimming pool to test the ergonomics.

Full-size testing, powered by an electric drill

The testing tank at Lancaster University

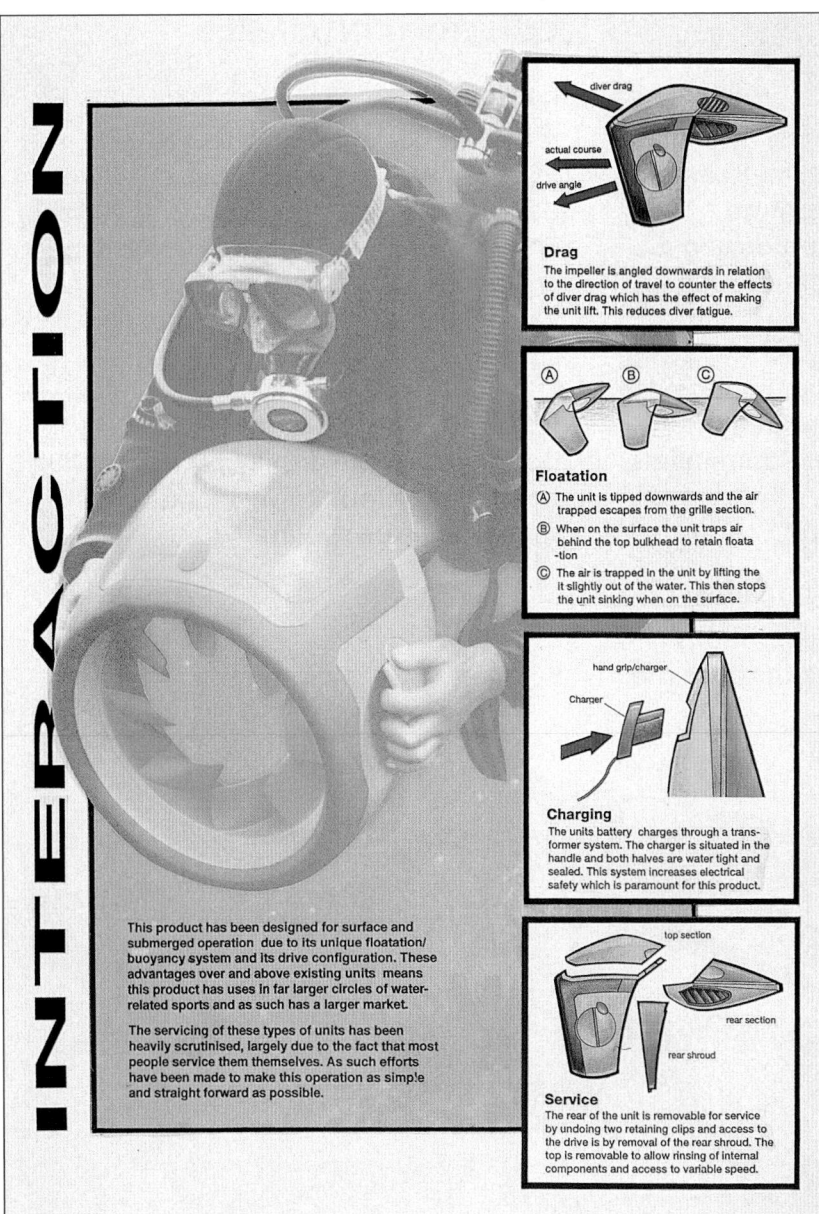

INTERACTION

Drag
The impeller is angled downwards in relation to the direction of travel to counter the effects of diver drag which has the effect of making the unit lift. This reduces diver fatigue.

Floatation
(A) The unit is tipped downwards and the air trapped escapes from the grille section.

(B) When on the surface the unit traps air behind the top bulkhead to retain floata-tion

(C) The air is trapped in the unit by lifting the it slightly out of the water. This then stops the unit sinking when on the surface.

Charging
The units battery charges through a trans-former system. The charger is situated in the handle and both halves are water tight and sealed. This system increases electrical safety which is paramount for this product.

Service
The rear of the unit is removable for service by undoing two retaining clips and access to the drive is by removal of the rear shroud. The top is removable to allow rinsing of internal components and access to variable speed.

This product has been designed for surface and submerged operation due to its unique floatation/ buoyancy system and its drive configuration. These advantages over and above existing units means this product has uses in far larger circles of water-related sports and as such has a larger market.

The servicing of these types of units has been heavily scrutinised, largely due to the fact that most people service them themselves. As such efforts have been made to make this operation as simple and straight forward as possible.

MANUFACTURE

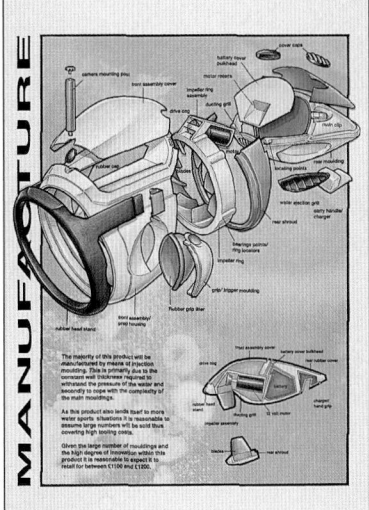

The form of the unit was developed through a series of models. A final appearance model was made, mainly from jelutong and MDF.

Design Briefs

JEWELLERY

Context

Jewellery designers sometimes experiment with materials such as card and paper to develop their ideas. Results from this type of approach can be exciting and have opened the way towards the idea of disposable or 'throwaway' jewellery. This low-cost, avant-garde jewellery should prove popular with the fashion-conscious teenager.

Brief

Design a range of low-cost, disposable jewellery. You may find it helpful to select a theme to provide inspiration for your ideas, for example

• Tribal

• Cyberspace

• Tropical

LIGHTING

Context

A leisure equipment company 'Meridian' require a new design for a small camping light. The company are intent on improving their image by producing a stylish, 'upmarket' range of products.

Brief

Design and make a working, lightweight, compact lighting unit. Your design should fulfil the following requirements. It must:

• use low voltage electricity

• present a stylish and exciting image

• fulfil the ergonomic considerations required for camping and outdoor use.

CUTLERY CONTAINER

Context

A plastics company specialising in injection moulding require a package design for a new range of picnic cutlery. This range of plastic picnicware will be promoted as an 'upmarket' design that will be distributed through popular stores.

Brief

Design a suitable display pack that will hold a set of four knives, forks, desert spoons and tea spoons.

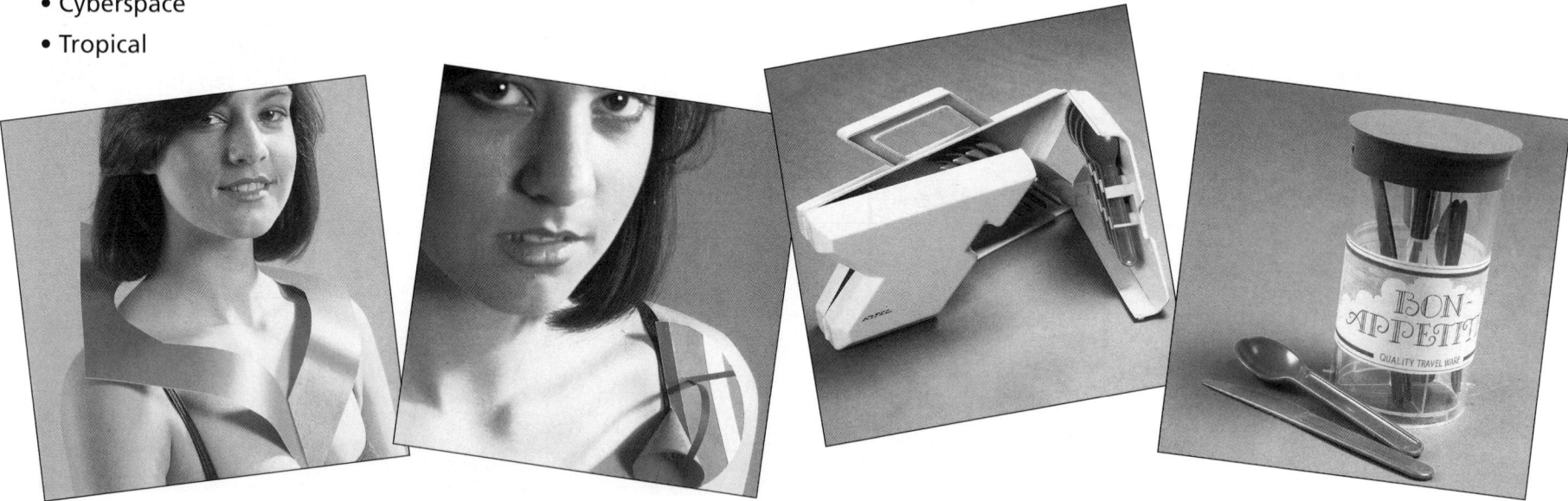

Design Briefs

SALES DISPLAY

Context

Point-of-sale displays in stores and supermarkets are used to promote ranges of products as diverse as perfume and kitchen knives. They are usually manufactured in card or thin plastic and can be transported as a 2D flatpack.

Brief

Design a card point-of-sale display for one of the following:

- an expensive aftershave
- a new CD or video
- vitamin tablets.

Your design should fold flat for transportation but allow for quick and easy assembly.

MONEY BOX

Context

A building society is starting a new children's savings account. Promotion of the new scheme includes a 'mailshot' with a pack of information and a free card 'money box'.

Brief

Develop an attractive image for the savings account and design and make the 'money box'. Your design should:

- identify and promote the building society
- encourage children to open an account and save with the scheme
- appeal to children of primary school age
- fold flat for postage and be easy to assemble.

TEMPORARY SHELTER

Context

When areas are hit by natural disasters, it is important to provide some form of temporary shelter. This must be inexpensive and easy to transport. It is also important that the shelter is quick and easy to assemble.

Brief

Using card as a modelling material, design a modular temporary shelter system which can be flat packed. Present your ideas as small-scale models.

Design Briefs

SUNGLASSES

Context

A fashion accessory firm are introducing their new season's range of sunglasses. The new glasses will appear under the brand name of 'Rio' and are directed at the teenage market.

Brief

Design a pair of sunglasses that would appeal to this young market. You should initially design and make a selection of card models which clearly convey the bright and exotic 'Rio' image. Select one of your ideas to develop into a wearable model.

(Modelling options could look at card, resistant materials or the use of CNC machining.)

COMMUNICATION

Context

Portable phones are now commonplace and video phones are no longer a futuristic fantasy. A number of professions, including the police and the military, are developing this technology to improve the ways in which they work. Video images from the scene of a crime can be relayed to a central office where they can be studied in detail at a later date.

Brief

Design a personal communication system which reflects the specialist needs of one of the following professions:

• community police officers

• mountaineers and explorers

• rescue teams.

Present your design as a full-size, non-working model.

BOTTLES AND JARS

Context

Manufacturers of food and drink place great importance on the packaging of their products. The colour, graphics and shape of the containers must be distinctive and eye-catching on the shelves. Certain products are instantly recognisable – the unmistakable shape and lettering on the *Coca-Cola* bottle is an example of this.

Brief

Design and make a concept model of a container for either 250 ml of 'Aruba', a Caribbean liqueur, or 500 g of 'Hobbs' low sugar, fruit conserve. The container should be complete with appropriate labels for a food product.

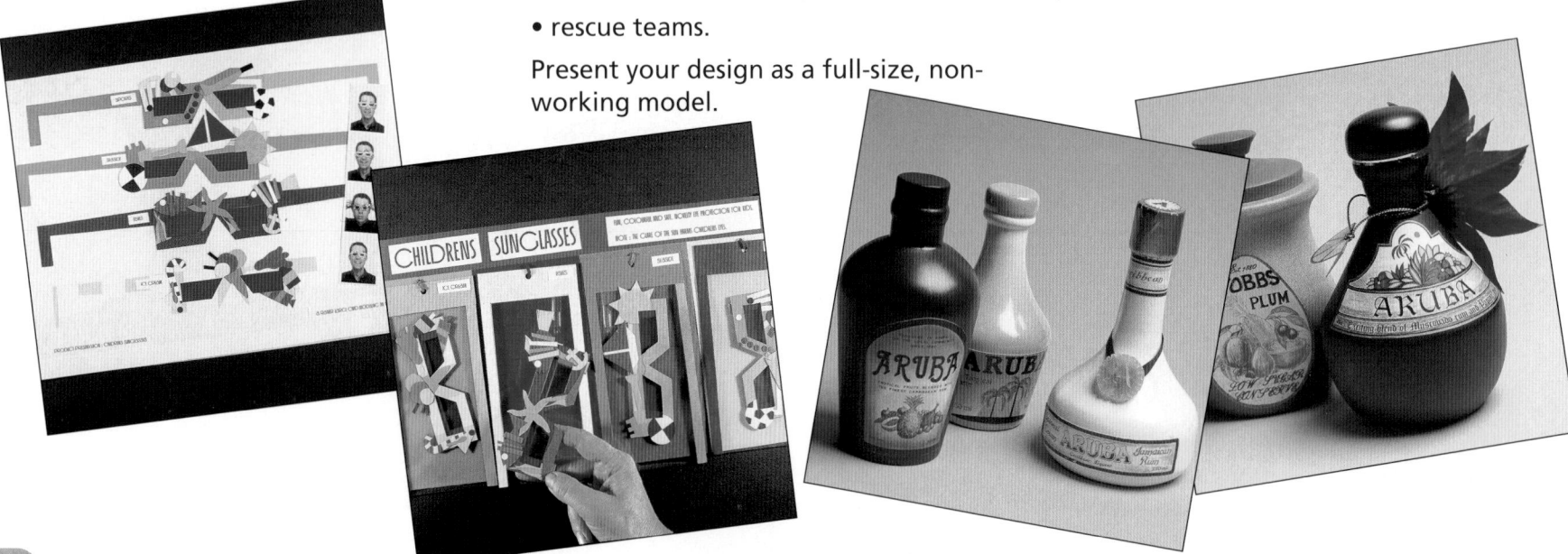

FIREWORKS

Context

Guy Fawkes is now more commonly celebrated at public gatherings where safer, organised displays replace individual fireworks such as the 'jumping jack' and 'banger'. Firework manufacturers are now producing a larger, more expensive type of firework for this new demand.

Brief

Develop ideas for a range of fireworks intended for use at public events (carnivals, weddings, Guy Fawkes' night, etc.). Present your ideas as dummy fireworks using dynamic graphics and colour to create an exciting product or to suggest how they will perform.

BADGES/BROOCHES

Context

Film companies promote new films through expensive advertising campaigns. These are becoming increasingly imaginative in an attempt to catch public interest.

Brief

Design an easily-recognisable symbol that can be used on promotional material (badges, stickers, buckles, etc.) for a film of your choice (the symbol used in *Batman* is an obvious example).

Use CNC machining to develop and make the final product.

TRAVEL IRON

Context

When going on holiday, clothes often become creased through being packed into bags and suitcases. If the holiday destination does not have facilities for ironing, this can be a problem.

Brief

Design and make a concept model of an iron that is suitable for taking on holiday. You will need to consider size, weight and ergonomics as well as the target group that it is designed to appeal to.

Design Briefs

CAMERA

Context

The technology involved in photographic equipment has, over recent years, advanced significantly. However, the styling of the camera has seen little change – many are still, basically, a rectangular box.

Brief

Design a camera body that:

- uses organic and natural forms as the starting point for your design
- takes ergonomic factors into consideration
- is suitable for use with a 35 mm film
- has an in-built flash unit.

MEN'S HAIRDRYER

Context

There has been considerable growth in the sale of men's toiletries. A number of companies have produced special packs containing a range of these products to exploit the market. One such company intends to extend this concept by producing a hairdryer designed specifically to appeal to men.

Brief

Design a hairdryer that appeals to the male market. Select one of the following target groups and design a hairdryer that would appeal specifically to that group.

- 18–30 sporty
- 30–45 business executive
- 15–25 seriously cool!

PORTABLE SEATING

Context

'ABC International' is to sponsor a series of outdoor sporting events and, as part of the promotional exercise, would like to offer a light, portable, folding seat. The events will include golfing, three-day events, etc. where the spectator may follow the action on foot.

Brief

Design a portable, folding seat considering the following points:

- the structure should be simple and easily assembled.
- the design should help to promote the sponsor 'ABC International'.

The word 'seat' refers to any structure that allows the user some degree of rest for the legs by supporting part or all of the body weight.

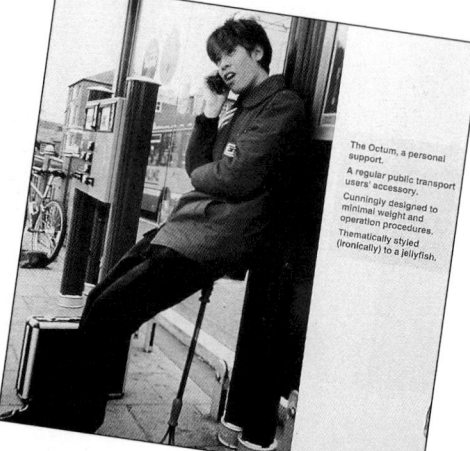

The Octum, a personal support.

A regular public transport users' accessory.

Cunningly designed to minimal weight and operation procedures.

Thematically styled (ironically) to a jellyfish.

MIRRORS

Context

A prominent design/craft gallery is to hold an exhibition to be titled 'REFLECTIONS'. It will feature designs using the decorative characteristics of natural timbers alongside the reflective qualities of mirrored glass as the main visual theme.

Brief

You are asked to produce an artefact for the exhibition which explores a combination of the materials specified.

NAVIGATION SYSTEM

Context

Finding your way with a map and compass can be difficult, particularly in bad weather where rain and high winds make it difficult to obtain the right information.

Brief

Design a compact, weather-proof product that is easy to carry and which will aid navigation. It should combine printed paper maps and a magnetic compass.

The product should be designed and priced to appeal to the domestic outdoor leisure market.

OUTDOOR SEATING

Context

Outdoor furniture is used in many areas around public buildings. Often it is of a standard shape and form rarely relating to the surroundings it is placed in.

Brief

Select a building or location which you feel would be improved by the addition of outdoor furniture. Using the architectural style of the building as a starting point, design seating that relates to the surroundings.

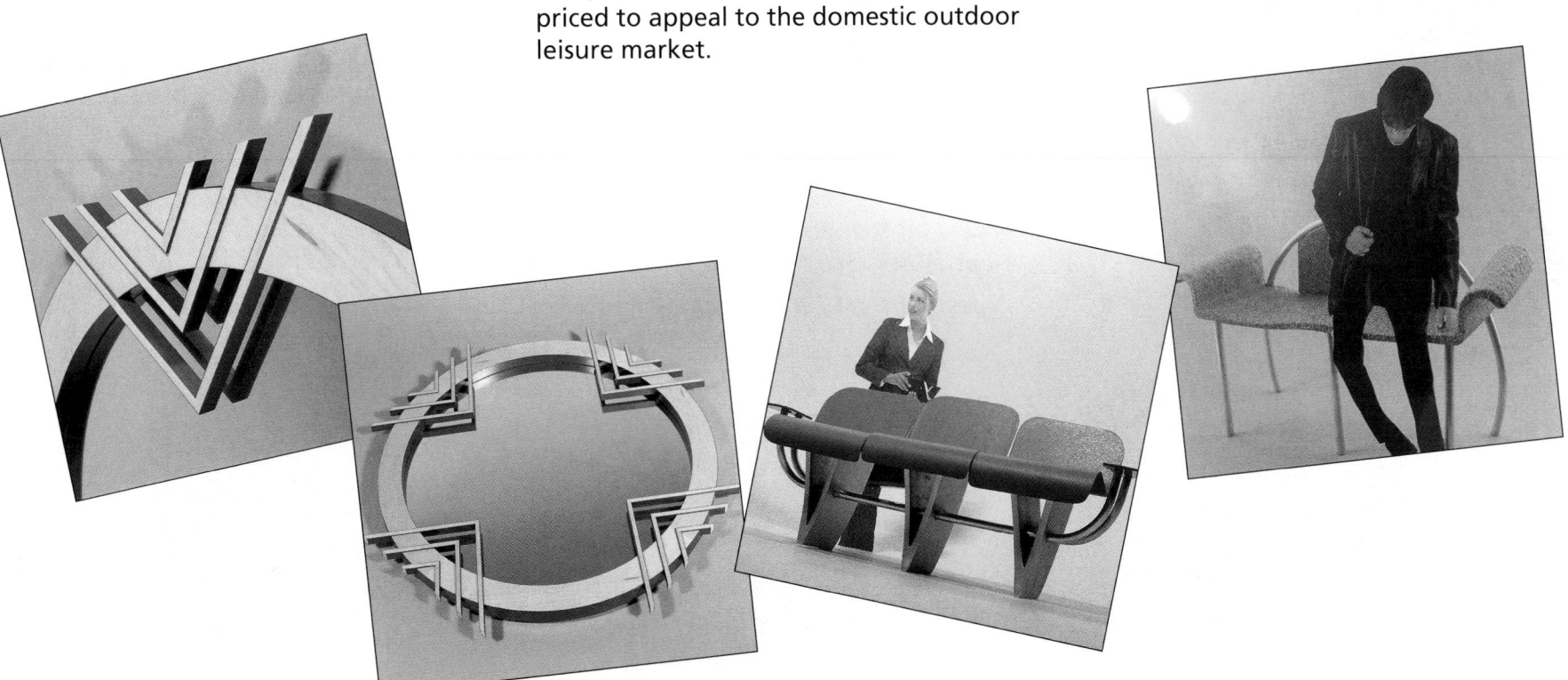

Design Briefs

COMPACT DISC PLAYER

Context

The music industry has witnessed a rapid growth in the development of the compact disc. The technology of a personal compact disc player allows for adventurous forms of styling.

Brief

Select a target group and produce a mood and image board.

PERSONALISED ID

Context

Some organisations require their employees to wear a form of identification card. In the majority of cases, this takes the form of a credit-card-sized plastic wallet with a paper insert bearing the wearer's name and photograph.

Brief

Design and make a wearable identity card for one of the areas listed below. Your design should reflect the image of the event or organisation involved. It should contain a photo, name, title of wearer, etc.

- A backstage pass for a rock concert.
- A field worker for Amnesty International.
- A pass for the pits at the Le Mans 24-Hour motor race.
- A pass for the New York Spring Fashion launch.

PLANT GIFT

Context

A traditional seed and bulb supplier has been struggling to survive in the existing economic climate. This is due to several factors including:

- the general decline in gardening as a hobby or pastime
- the ready availability of pre-grown plants and seedlings.

Brief

Use brainstorming to establish ideas for new plant-based products that could help boost sales for the company. Design and make an appealing gift item that could form part of a new line in horticultural products.

CULTURAL

Context

'VISIONS' design consultancy specialise in promoting major national events such as the Grand National and Henley Regatta.

Brief

As a member of the design team at 'VISIONS', you have been asked to produce a 3D invitation card for one of the events listed.

- The Henley Regatta
- Wimbledon Tennis Tournament
- The Grand National
- The Clothes Show
- The Glastonbury Rock Festival
- The Milk Race

WINDOW DISPLAY

Context

Department stores use dynamic, eye-catching window displays to promote sales of new products. The display must obviously attract attention and reflect the image of the products displayed.

Brief

Design a window display that will incorporate one, or a combination, of the following effects:

- movement or lighting

You may select a product from the following list:

- 'Kaleidoscope' – a non-permanent hair colour
- 'Dazzle' – toothpaste
- 'Revive' – sparkling mineral water
- 'Luminaire' – pastel shade light bulbs
- 'Grow-it' – a fitness food for plants.

LIFEGUARD TOWER

Context

Lifeguard rescue is an important aspect of beach life which is often taken for granted. Some beaches are particularly dangerous and, during the holiday season, need to be overseen by a permanent team of lifeguards.

Brief

Following research into the tasks undertaken by lifeguards, design a lifeguard tower that will give maximum practicality to the user. Main features to consider are the viewing point and structural stability. It should also be styled to contribute rather than detract from the landscape.

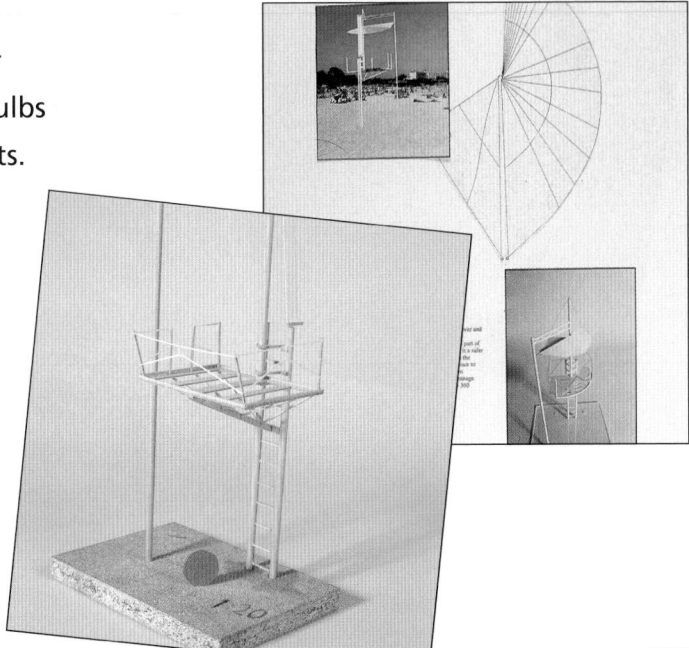

Design Briefs

PERSONALISED JEWELLERY

Context

Jewellery is a popular choice of gift. It can be made more personal by having a piece designed (especially) for an individual.

Brief

Design and make a clothes fastener. This can be a buckle, clip, button or indeed any device which would hold clothing together. It should be functional, attractive and appealing to a particular celebrity or character from a favourite film or book e.g. Madonna, Frankenstein, Cleopatra, etc.

SOLDERING IRON

Context

With the development of technology courses in schools, the use of the soldering iron is increasing. Its design, however, has developed little in terms of safety, ergonomics and appearance. Clearly there is need to reappraise the existing product in order to meet the needs of its new user.

Brief

Design a soldering iron for use by a young age group (11–15). Pay particular attention to ergonomics and safety.

SCALPEL-BLADE HOLDER

Context

The scalpel blade is a cheap, yet effective, cutting device which is used in many professions (hospital surgeons, graphic designers, crafts, etc.). The type of holder available for them is limited and there is scope for developing new designs.

Brief

Design a scalpel-blade holder with an emphasis on user considerations and appearance. You may develop a new principle of operation or use for the blade but this is not a chief requirement of the project.

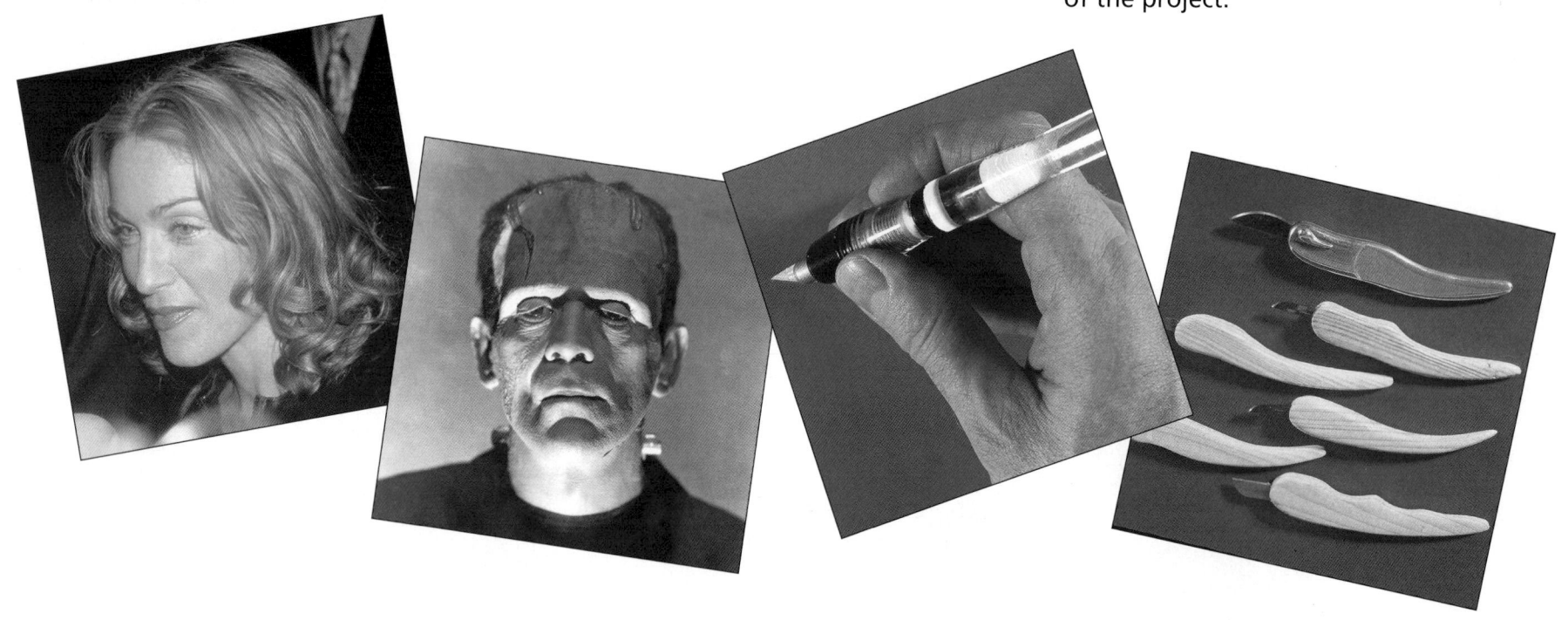

Materials Information

MATERIALS	DESCRIPTION	USES
Manufactured boards (wood-based)	Available in standard sheet size (2.4m x 1.2m) and thickness (6 mm, 9 mm, 12 mm, etc.)	General purpose, structures
Pine (red deal)	Quite strong; fairly easy to cut and shape. Its open grain can make it difficult to finish/paint	Frameworks, block models
Lime and jelutong (hardwood)	Quite strong; easy to cut and shape; allows for finer surface finish.	Block models, mould making
Balsa wood	Very light and easy to work; fragile	Lightweight structures, rapid models and small–scale models
Aluminium	Light; easy to cut, shape and cast	Structures, foil useful for scale models
Acrylic	Thermoplastic (deforms with heat); brittle; easy to work and finish; available in a range of colours and finishes	Press and drape moulding, mechanisms, curved components
ABS (acrylonitrile butadiene styrene)	Thermoplastic; available in a range of colours; strong and tough; easy to cut and shape	Frameworks, mechanical parts, scale modelling
Polystyrene	Thermoplastic; available in a range of colours; works easily; flexible	Vacuum forming, can be laminated and carved for detailed components
High–density polystyrene foam	Available as sheet or block; light; very easy to cut and shape	Rapid modelling, packaging
PVC (poly vinyl chloride)	Thermoplastic; works easily; flexible	Fabrication, tubing
Nylon	Thermoplastic; strong and tough; self–lubricating; machines well	Small components, mechanisms

Materials Information

MATERIALS	DESCRIPTION	USES
Polyester resin*	Thermosetting; liquid that sets solid by adding hardener; wide range of colours	Casting components, fibre–glass moulding
Foam board	Foam sandwiched between card; stiff; light; cuts easily	Interior and architectural modelling
Card	Available in various thicknesses, colours and surface finishes; easy to cut, bend and fold.	Pop-ups (less than 300 microns), cartons, packaging (350–400 and microns) and point-of-sale display (more than 650 microns)

ADHESIVES	USES
Acrylic cement e.g. Tensol*	Acrylic to acrylic
Contact adhesive e.g. Thixofix*	General purpose
Epoxy resin e.g. Araldite *	Metals, some plastics and dissimilar materials e.g. wood to metal
Natural latex e.g. Copydex *	Textiles and expanded polystyrene
PVA e.g. Evostik resin W	Timber–based materials, textiles and expanded polystyrene
PVC e.g. Bartol *	PVC to PVC
Synthetic resin e.g. Cascamite	Timber–based materials
Cyanoacrylate e.g. Super glue*	Most materials
Hot glue gun*	Most materials, rapid joining
Double-sided tape	Most materials especially card/paper

Use in well-ventilated areas. Follow manufacturer's instructions.

FINISHES

Sanding sealer – Sealant for porous surfaces. Apply prior to paint or lacquer

Primer (general, metal etch, plastic) Use as a base for finishing coat.

Cellulose paint – Available in spray cans in a wide variety of finishing colours

Emulsion paint – Basic finish for foam and MDF

Acrylic varnish (water based) – For timber based models. Apply up to three coats

Wood stains – Used to colour timbers. Available in a wide range of colours.

Metal/plastic polish e.g. Brasso – For burnishing surface of material

Prepare all surfaces prior to finishing

Glossary

2 Dimensional (2D)
An image that shows only two of its three dimensions. For example, length and width but no depth

3 Dimensional (3D)
An image that shows all three dimensions of an object – length, width and depth

American Styling Wax
A clay-like material used for modelling

Car-body filler
An epoxy-based filler which, when mixed with a hardener, will set hard. Useful for filling in defects and surface blemishes

Computer aided design (CAD)
Designing, through computer use, 2D and 3D models

Computer aided manufacture (CAM)
Manufacture by computer-controlled machinery

Concept
An idea or impression

Ergonomics
Design considerations that take people's actions into account

Extrude
To stretch or pull out

Facsimile
A copy or reflection of an object

Gouache
A water-based paint that is not as transparent as water-colour paint

LEGO
A modelling kit which uses plastic 'bricks' that can be linked together

LEGO Technic
As above, but includes gears, levers, linkages, motors, etc.

Mass production
The process of making many copies of the same thing

Meccano
A modelling kit which uses metal components that can be joined together with nuts and bolts

MDF
Medium density fibreboard

Orthographic
An engineering drawing method of showing a three-dimensional object by projecting three views of it (front, side and plan)

Perspective
A 3D drawing method which produces a realistic image of an object

Polystyrene foam
A high-density foam which is easy to model.

Prototype
Models that represent the finished article, made to test ideas

Rubberised paint
A special type of paint that gives a rubber texture when dry

Sanding sealer
A cellulose-based liquid used to seal porous surfaces. Prevents paint absorption.

Stereolithography
An industrial modelling process which uses a 3D computer image to make a solid model through the use of a laser and liquid resin

Texture
The surface quality of a material

Vanishing point
A point where perspective lines converge

Wireframe
A transparent image of a 3D object made up of lines and points

Index